Pioneer Churches of Springfield, Missouri

Pioneer Churches of Springfield, Missouri

Celebrating More Than a Century of Service

Paul W. Bass
and
Cecilia M. Chittenden

Acclaim Press™
MORLEY, MISSOURI

Acclaim Press
— Your Next Great Book —

P.O. Box 238
Morley, MO 63767
(573) 472-9800
www.acclaimpress.com

Book Design: Rodney Atchley
Cover Design: M. Frene Melton

Library of Congress Control Number: 2017908946
ISBN: 978-1-942613-71-8 / 1-942613-71-7
First Printing 2017
Printed in the United States of America
10 9 8 7 6 5 4 3 2 1

This publication was produced using available information.
The publisher regrets it cannot assume responsibility for errors or omissions.

Cover Photo: Christ Episcopal Church (601 East Walnut Street)

Contents

Authors' Notes

Why write a book about Springfield church history?

The idea for this book originated after examining the numerous notebooks about Springfield history collected by Robert Bowers, a local Springfield resident. These notebooks contained several old photos and newspaper articles about some of the churches celebrating their centennials. Questions were raised about when they were organized and how many churches in Springfield were at least one hundred years old. Were there enough churches to warrant writing a collective, historical account? In preliminary research it was discovered, first, there was no current book regarding the early churches organized in Springfield, and second, there were lists of churches organized before 1915. Some of these were still active, some were no longer in existence, and some were omitted from those early lists.

How did we choose which churches to write about?

It became apparent after the preliminary research and several interviews with Springfield historians that we would need to establish standards of qualification for choosing which churches to include in a book. We decided on three main qualifications:

1. The church must have been organized before 1915.
2. The church must be currently active.
3. The church must be within the current Springfield city limits.

It was decided, after getting into the early research, that further limitations were necessary. A definition of terms within the standards was needed. We decided that the word "church" would be interpreted to mean any group of religious adherents organized for worship and ministry. The word "organization" would be understood to mean an official declaration by the adherents of its founding. The term "city limits" would be understood as the 2015 declared city limits of Springfield, Missouri.

What were other considerations in the selection of churches?

It was important to look beyond the labels of being Christian or orthodox. The definitions would allow for inclusion, instead of exclusion, of any religious group researched. There is great value to any community in having a tolerance of all religious faiths represented. Questions of whether any group meets the standards of orthodoxy are highly subjective, not relative, and not appropriate for the purpose of this book.

What resources did we use in research?

As previously mentioned, the collection of Robert Bowers' notebook articles was the launching pad. The public libraries were helpful in discovering books about Springfield history, in general, with listings of the early churches. Many of the churches, celebrating centennial observations, produced written documentation of their histories, which were invaluable in developing their stories. A number of churches had historians and/or a history committee that were so gracious to meet with us and share materials. The materials used in research are listed after each church story and at the end the book.

What was discovered in our research?

First, with great surprise, we discovered that there were more churches in Springfield that met our standards than originally anticipated. Second, that nearly every denomination experienced divisions causing some of the Springfield churches to align with one side or the other during the Civil War. Third, that many of the churches established other new churches in the city. Fourth, that some of the churches changed names because of new locations or mergers. Fifth, that Springfield has been blessed with a variety of different religious beliefs and has experienced a community of respect and tolerance.

What were some of the challenges faced in researching this book?

First, there were discrepancies in some of the resources. Historians can make mistakes. When two historians offer differing dates of organization, or when a church publication offers differing organizational dates than other references, there is a mistake somewhere. Church members' oral histories can also offer a set of differing dates and claims. Second, changes in a church's identity can produce some interesting challenges. That identity change may involve a new location, a name change, a denominational split or a denominational change. Third, it is easy to become overwhelmed with the magnitude of the research required for a credible book. As the journey of a thousand miles begins with one step, the tasks for this book begins with one church at a time. Although there was an initial idealistic calendar plan for the completion of this book, it was necessary to adjust and offer flexibility with accuracy of information becoming a greater priority than just completing content on a very personalized schedule.

What do we hope this book will accomplish?

It is our desire that this book will be a testimony of God's blessing on people united for worship and ministry. It is hoped that it will be an updated and accurate history of the development of religious activities in Springfield. It is also hoped that the book is a fair picture of each church listed, and demonstrates a respect for their history and current leadership.

Disclaimer

It must be noted, just as we have found in the early church histories of Springfield, that historians do make mistakes. If we have omitted any church or included any church incorrectly in the list, we apologize and submit that the error was not intentional.

Paul William Bass and Cecelia M. Chittenden
Summer 2017

Timeline

(Currently operating churches listed in **BOLD** *print)*

1831 James River Fork of the White Water Mission
Methodist Episcopal, 1833
Grace United Methodist, 1864 (northern)
St. Paul's Methodist, 1861 (southern)
Downtown Church, 2015
1834 First Christian Church (Disciples of Christ)
merged with **South Street Christian Church,** 1918
1844 **First Cumberland Presbyterian Church**
Calvary Presbyterian Church, 1849 (new school)
First Presbyterian Church, 1860 (old school)
merged into **First & Calvary Presbyterian Church**, 1930
1847 Wilson's Creek Chapel, 1847
Pitts Chapel United Methodist Church, 1911
1852 **First Baptist Church**
1859 **Christ (Protestant) Episcopal Church**
1865 **Gibson Chapel Presbyterian Church**
1867 Second Baptist Church
Washington Avenue Baptist Church, 1904
Turning Point, 2016
1867 Tatum Chapel
Freedom Church, 1908
1868 **Immaculate Conception Catholic Church**
1869 Union Evangelical (Congregational) Church
(also known as First Congregational Church)
1873 Dever Benton Avenue Methodist Episcopal Church
1874 Benton Avenue A.M.E. Church (closed doors July 2015)
1876 Zion Primitive Baptist Church
1882 First Swedish Baptist Church

1882 **Sacred Heart Catholic Church**
1883 Central Congregational Church **(Drury College)**
1884 German Congregational Church
1885 First Methodist Church
1885 Second Presbyterian Church
1885 **Westminster Presbyterian Church**
1885 North Springfield Baptist Church
  Robberson Avenue Baptist Church, 1919
    Second Baptist Church, 1945
1885 **Salvation Army**
1886 Mount Eagle Colored Baptist Church
1886 **St. John's (Protestant) Episcopal Church**
1886 **Campbell (Street) United Methodist Church**
1886 Swedish Congregational Church
1886 **Macedonia Baptist Church**
1887 **South Street Christian Church**
1887 St. John's (German) Evangelical Church
  St. John's United Church of Christ, 1957
1889 Daily Memorial Methodist Church
1889 Boulevard Methodist Church
  Mount Carmel United Methodist Church, 1920
1889 Washington Avenue Church
  Central Christian Disciples of Christ Church, 1902
1889 Third Baptist Church
  East Avenue Baptist Church, 1890
    National Heights Baptist Church, 1979
1890 Temple Israel
1891 **Grant (Street) Avenue Baptist Church**
1891 Boulevard Baptist Church
  Pythian (Home) Avenue Baptist Church, 1912
    Just for Jesus Church, 2016
1892 Springfield Avenue Presbyterian Church
1892 **St. Joseph's Catholic Church**
1895 Ray Chapel Baptist Church
  Hamlin Memorial Baptist Church, 1908
1896 Reorganized Latter Day Saints Church, Central Congregation
  Community of Christ, 2001
1899 **Seventh Day Adventist**

1899 **First Church of Christ, Scientist**
1902 Vesta Avenue Methodist Episcopal Church
1904 Church of God Seventh Day
1905 Metropolitan Colored Baptist Church
1907 **Woodland Heights Presbyterian Church**
1907 **Central Assembly of God Church (Evangel College)**
1908 Pilgrim Congregational Church
1908 **St. Agnes Catholic Parish**
1910 **Trinity Lutheran Church**
1911 Seventh Baptist Church
    National Boulevard Baptist Church, 1934
1911 Johnson and Dale Church of Christ
    Kansas Expressway Church of Christ, 1977
1912 Mt. Zion Colored Church
1913 Sunset Baptist Church
    Northwest Baptist Church, 1935
1914 First Freewill Baptist Church
1915 Westside Baptist Church
    Immanuel Baptist Church, 1930
1915 Forest Hills Church
    Walnut Street Christian Church, 1947

Introduction

Rev. James Slavens spent long, lonely hours in the saddle for many days each week. He had become familiar with the wilderness wagon trails he had to follow and the few places along the way where he could stop for a night's rest. He used the time spent in the saddle to reflect, prepare and plan. For this circuit-riding minister, there was much to consider.

He reflected on his ministerial calling, his ministry experiences, and his current mission challenge. He reminded himself of his calling to the ministry and the two-year trial period requested by the Methodist Episcopal National Conference in 1830. The conference listed his acceptance and ordination in 1832. Rev. James Slavens was assigned at a conference meeting in Cape Girardeau, Missouri, to the James Fork of the White River Mission. It was a large territory covering an area 100 miles north to south, from about Bolivar to Branson, and 200 miles east to west.

Slavens also spent his saddle time preparing for his teaching, preaching and numerous records and reports (oral and written). He was accountable to one of the two superintendents in Missouri and was to make regular reports to the conference authorities.

Slavens would also use his time planning for financial support, finding new converts, establishing church starts and fostering church growth. He led numerous home Bible studies that would evolve into organized churches. There are records of early weddings he performed. He was dependent upon the kindness and hospitality of families he encountered along the wagon trails. There were numerous churches organized and eventually several of the area's earliest church buildings were constructed under his ministry.

From this challenging foundation, other ministers would be called and assigned and new churches would be organized. The growing population centered around Springfield, Missouri, would grow into a broad mixture of denominations and worship centers. By 1915, there were over fifty-eight organized worship centers listed within the city limits of Springfield. Of those listed, thirty-nine would still be active in 2017. Some of those established during that 100-plus-year period had name changes, splits or denominational realignments.

The spiritual impact those groups would have on the city of Springfield is difficult to measure. More important, was the significance of these groups upon the thousands of individuals calling Springfield their home.

Pioneer Churches of Springfield, Missouri

Celebrating More Than a Century of Service

Chapter One

Pre-Civil War

Historical Notes

The Osage and Kickapoo Indian tribes, of the current southwest Missouri area, encountered the first white explorers around 1800. Twenty years later, the first white settlers came to the area, mostly from Tennessee. On August 1, 1821, Missouri was admitted to the Union as a compromise slave state. With a slow but steady migration of settlers from Tennessee and Kentucky, the area in the new state began to develop. In 1833, Greene County was officially established. By 1835, about 500 people lived in the Springfield area. Five years later, on February 19, 1838, the city of Springfield, Missouri, was incorporated. In that same year, the Cherokees were forcibly marched through the city on the Trail of Tears on what was known as the Old Wire Road. On April 14, 1841, the University of Missouri opened as the first state university west of the Mississippi River. The first United States census of 1844 listed the population of Greene County at 5,372. In 1846, a group known as the Springfield Volunteers, answered the call to fight in the Mexican War. On December 20, 1847, St. Louis was connected with the East Coast by telegraph.

By 1852, the city had grown and "contained five stores, two or three blacksmith shops, a bank, a courthouse, a schoolhouse and a saloon. Coffee was selling for 12.5 cents per pound; sugar, 10 cents per pound; and bacon, 8 cents per pound." Only two churches held services: Methodist and Presbyterian.

By the late 1850s, Springfield's population had grown to about 2,000. In 1852, a Baptist church was organized and experienced steady growth. In 1858, a steam-powered planing mill began operation. Communication advances were made with stagecoach mail delivery and telegraph wires. The town and county spent $36,000 for a new courthouse and jail.

Earliest Church Activities

Although the area was not known for its religious fervor, some of the early settlers brought their religious faith and practices with them. Several itinerant preachers were assigned to the new territory as circuit riders. As early as 1829, there was mention of the Mt. Zion Church. Such groups were mostly home churches without a permanent building site. Records from the Methodist Episcopal annual conference of 1831, listed the establishment of the James River Fork of the White River Mission. Two years later at the annual conference, Rev. James Slavens was assigned as the official minister to the area. There is also mention of a First Christian Church, established in 1832. It was thought to have later merged with the South Street Christian Church. Springfield historical records indicate that the first church building in the city was built in 1833. It was the First Methodist Episcopal Church. The building was later shared with the Cumberland Presbyterians. A historical marker was placed near the church building site in 1921. Known as Marker Number Nine, located at the entrance of Silver Springs Park, it reads as follows:

585 feet southwest, first church Methodist Episcopal in southwest Missouri was located in 1833. Size 18 X 20 feet, built of logs, puncheon floor and seats. Cost 18 dollars. Rev. Jas. H. Slavens, M.D., first pastor over White River and St. Francis districts. 100 by 200 miles in extent. Marker erected by the Springfield Episcopal and Methodist Episcopal churches South, 1921.

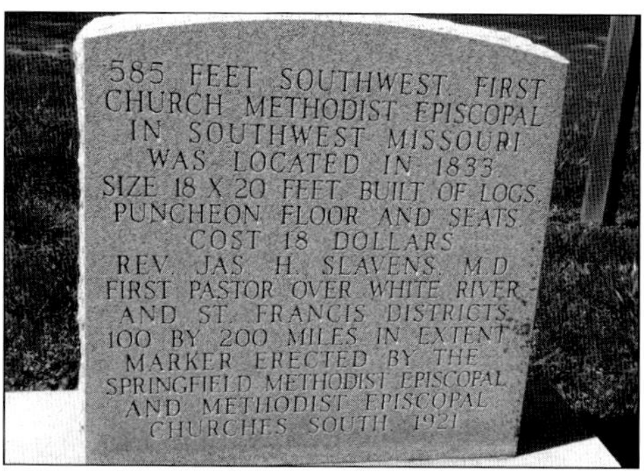

Some of these earliest churches would continue in their ministry role to the present day, after several name changes. Nearly a decade after the building of this first church structure, major denominational splits began to occur in the nation, the state and locally in Springfield. Missouri, as a compromise state, was born in the controversy of the slavery issue. A majority of the residents of Springfield, being from Tennessee and Kentucky, were southern sympathizers, defending the issue of slavery. The controversy was felt in the local, established churches among the Baptists, Methodists and Presbyterians. Churches split and new churches were established along the lines of sympathies over the slavery issue. It is sadly reported that some of the local church divisions created were not healed until 1939.

Currently Operating Churches

Methodist Episcopal Church, 1833
St. Paul's Methodist Church, 1861
Downtown Church, 2015
Grace Methodist Church, 1864
First Christian Church (Disciples of Christ), 1834
(merged with **South Street Christian Church**, 1918)
First Cumberland Presbyterian Church, 1844, May 19
Calvary Presbyterian Church, 1849 (new school)
First Presbyterian Church, 1860 (old school)
First & Calvary Presbyterian Church, 1930, July 10
Pitts Chapel United Methodist Church, 1847
First Baptist Church, 1852
Christ (Protestant) Episcopal Church, 1859

Springfield's society was impacted by the growing pioneer churches. However, the status of Springfield's early society also had an impact on the local churches. In the first half of the nineteenth century, Springfield's society reflected the national struggle over the issue of slavery and states' rights. The earliest denominational churches in Springfield were deeply affected by the divisions over the slavery issue. The earliest Methodist Episcopal church was becoming divided between those with northern or southern sympathies. This division led to disputes over the building, finances and leadership. The northern sympathizers, in the minority, would eventually establish the Grace Methodist Church. The southern sympathizers would eventually form the St. Paul's Methodist Church. The history of these two churches are intertwined and originated from the early Methodist Episcopal Church.

Grace Methodist Church, 1879

Grace Church, 1842

The 1833 Methodist Episcopal Church building was named the Kickapoo Meeting House. It was built on land deeded to the U.S. Government by the Kickapoo Indians. The church later shared its building with Presbyterians, who met on Sunday afternoons. A second building was constructed in 1842, closer to town, at what is today the southwest corner of South Avenue and Walnut Street.

There were divisions among the membership over the use and development of the new building. Further divisions came to the forefront because of the slavery issue. Disorganization resulted and the church united with the Missouri Conference and formed the Methodist-Episcopal Church, South. A smaller remnant of northern supporters, with help from former pastor James Slavens, organized in secret because of physical persecution.

The Methodist-Episcopal Church, South, began construction, in 1858, of a grand two-story building with a large spire. Because of the growing discontent and economic challenges, the building was not completed when the Civil War broke out. Both Union and Confederate forces gained control of the uncompleted church building for use at various times as an arsenal, supply depot, hospital and stable. During the Civil War period, there were no regularly-held church services in the city.

In 1864, attempts were made to reorganize the Methodist-Episcopal Church, North. The group met in a building used by the Calvary Presbyterian Church. After the war, the federal government gave the unfinished church building to the Methodist-Episcopal Church, North and a title was purchased from the Methodist-Episcopal Church, South. Membership grew and funds were raised to complete construction of

Bentley Chapel, 1879

the building. A scheduled building dedication was planned, but on May 28, 1868, a tornado caused significant damage to the building. Lacking funds, the group was forced to abandon the building. They met, with permission in the U.S. Courthouse, on the public square. The damaged building was sold back to the Methodist-Episcopal Church, South for the amount of the remaining debt.

In less than a year, during 1869, a lot was purchased on South and Pershing Streets and a plain brick building was purchased. The group was named Bentley Chapel in honor of Rev. J.J. Bentley, who helped the small group through difficult challenges. In 1879, a building addition was constructed and the name was changed to Grace Methodist-Episcopal Church.

The congregation experienced continued growth, filling the worship facility. New construction began on the same lot and was attached to the old Bentley Chapel building. The new brick and neo-Gothic structure was completed in 1895. The church experienced unusually rapid growth and outreach. An Estey pipe organ was purchased in 1908.

Within a decade, there was a need for a larger church facility. A lot was purchased on the southeast corner of Jefferson Avenue and Cherry Street. The old facility was razed and many of the sanctuary items were sold to help pay for the new facility, a "suppressed" Gothic style building. Worship and education facilities were completed in June 1921.

Grace Methodist Church, 1921

The building was the largest church in the city and in the Methodist Conference.

The church experienced continued growth until the Great Depression years of the 1930s. Like so many institutions and families, financial hardships caused difficulty in meeting expense payments. The church remained seriously troubled until, in what seemed like divine intervention, a dove appeared in the church office. In 1937, a new, inspired financial campaign successfully eliminated all indebtedness.

Like many mainstream denominations, the church continued growth in membership and facility improvements throughout the 1940s and 1950s. A serious division within the membership occurred in the 1960s when the church growth required some form of facility expansion. Most of the members wanted to build an attached three-story education building. A minority wanted to move the entire church plant to donated land at Battlefield and Fremont Streets. After continued de-

Grace Methodist Church, 2017

liberation, the church voted in 1964 to build the education wing. Many members left the church after the vote. Other disagreements over facility improvements caused additional members to leave the fellowship.

A major sanctuary renovation took place in 1979, with the addition of a newly-commissioned pipe organ. The aging church membership had difficulty attracting younger families throughout the 1980s and 1990s. Failed programs led to the decision to merge with the nearby St. Paul's United Methodist Church in 2005. The merged congregations adopted the name of the First United Methodist Church.

Continued century-old issues of what the church should be caused the dissolution of the merger two years later. On July 1, 2007, the breakaway congregation was reorganized as the Grace United Methodist Church.

Current Information

600 South Jefferson, Springfield, Missouri
(417) 869-0765
www.yourgraceplace.org

Resources Used

Fairbanks, Jonathan and Tuck, Clyde Edwin. *Past and Present of Greene County Missouri, Volume 1*, A.W. Bowen and Company: Indianapolis, Indiana, 1915

Images of America, Springfield, 1830-1930, page 27

"Neighbors unite," Springfield News-Leader, October 1, 2005

St. Paul's United Methodist Church, 1831-1982, One Hundred and Fiftieth Anniversary booklet

www.thelibrary.org/lochist/postcards/grace_methodist.cfm

www.thelibrary.org/lochist/history/paspres/ch19py2.html

www.yourgraceplace.org/our-history/

Downtown Church, 2015

(St. Paul's United Methodist Church)

The history of the Downtown Church originates from the early Methodist Episcopal Church and is closely entwined with the Grace United Methodist Church. Within the original Methodist Episcopal Church, divisions began to develop over two issues. First, was the question of what the church should be. Some favored a high church with appropriate facility and worship style. Others favored a more socially-minded, ministry church. The second divisive issue was the question of slavery and states' rights. The church officially split in 1844. With many members having roots in Tennessee and Kentucky, the majority of the members favored high church and pro-slavery positions. This group developed into the Methodist-Episcopal Church, South of Springfield, Missouri.

A new church building was planned on the same site at the corner of South Avenue and Walnut Street in 1858. The church membership had grown to over two hundred and subscriptions were raised for a new building. By the spring of 1861, the church was incomplete, but the basement was used with a worship area designated for slaves. Sadly, after the Civil War was declared in April 1861, the church was confiscated by both sides of the conflict and used for various purposes.

During the war, regular worship services were abandoned. Only an interdenominational service was held in the city, led by a chaplain of the Union Army, Frederick H. Wines, at Calvary Presbyterian Church on the corner of Jefferson Avenue and Elm Street. After the war, the victorious Union forces allowed the Methodist Episcopal Church, North, to assume control of the unfinished church structure. Progress was made to complete the facility. However, when it was near completion, with a dedication service being planned, a terrible storm destroyed part of the building. With insufficient funds to repair the damage, the Methodist Episcopal Church, South, in 1868, was able to purchase the church with its damage and indebtedness. After many bazaars and dinners, funds were raised to repair and complete the church structure.

Significant church growth was experienced in the 1870s and 1880s. Additionally, needed repairs and facility improvements were made. The church now had a membership of over three hundred.

In 1886, at the suggestion of the pastor, Rev. W.B. Palmore, the name of the church was officially changed to St. Paul's Methodist Church.

At the beginning of the twentieth century, there was a need for further expansion. A decision was made to sell the current building site and relocate to build a bigger facility. The new site selected was on the northeast corner of Walnut Street and Jefferson Avenue. On June 26, 1904, the dedication of the new church was held. Disputes arose over the furnishings in the sanctuary and further indebtedness. Avoiding a disruptive church division, very generous, personal donations were made to purchase the furnishings in question.

During the 1910s and the 1920s, the church continued to experience significant growth of membership as well as facility improvements. Membership increased to almost 400. The improvements included a new parsonage, electric lighting, a three-story education building addition and the Centenary, which was a residence for homeless girls. The church also helped to establish the new St. Luke's Church. In 1916, the church historian was able to collect $2,150 from the federal government for damages to the former church property during the Civil War.

The 1930s found the church affected by the Great Depression era. The church kept itself afloat with careful and prayerful watch over finances. The church members, though, were greatly affected by the national depression. It was reported that morale was low among the people and the church staff.

St. Paul's Methodist Church, 1904

In 1939, a great union took place within the Methodist bodies. The Methodist Protestant Church, the Methodist Episcopal Church and the Methodist Episcopal Church, South, all merged. The church's name was now the St. Paul's Methodist Church. Another merger in 1968 with the Evangelical United Brethren Church saw the church's name changed again to the St. Paul's United Methodist Church.

The longest serving pastor was Dr. Robert Arbaugh. He served from 1958-1981. During his tenure, facility renovations were made and adjacent land purchased for parking. Other churches established through St. Paul's, in addition to St. Luke's, were Guy Street, Dale Street and King's Highway.

The aging membership of the church found a decrease in membership and attendance in the 1990s and early 2000s. The church merged in 2005 with the also aging Grace Methodist Church. The merger lasted only two years before the Grace congregation dissolved the union and left. Through deaths, retirement, relocations and the inability to attract younger families, the church faced a serious decision about their purpose and identity. Several attempts at innovative ministry failed. The church was now meeting in the basement with less than one hundred members.

Assessment by the remaining faithful attendees was realistic. One member commented, "We had more money than we had people." Inspite of a generous endowment that would keep the church in operation for several years, the membership did not want to be the last of a dying church.

St. Paul's Methodist Church, 2017

After joining forces with members of the local Wesley Downtown Mission in 2014, the two groups felt led to organize into the Downtown Church. That same year, Lori Lampert came to the Downtown Church to revitalize its mission and identity in the community. The congregation renewed its calling to minister to the local community. The services are informal and the congregation is now a mixture of young and old. Hope is high for the future of the church since they have rediscovered their true purpose.

Current Information

413 East Walnut Street
(417) 866-4326
www.the downtown.church

Resources Used

"Downtown Church Thriving," *Springfield News-Leader*, November 14, 2015, page 1C

State Historical Society of Missouri, St. Paul's Methodist Church (Springfield, Mo.). 886 Newsletter, 1939. One folder.

St. Paul's United Methodist Church, 1831-1982, One Hundred and Fiftieth Anniversary booklet

www.shresearch@umsystem.edu, State Historical Society of Missouri, R-St. Paul's Methodist Church (Springfield, Mo.), 886, Newsletter, 1939, one folder

Fairbanks, Jonathan and Tuck, Clyde Edwin. *Past and Present of Greene County Missouri, Volume 1*, A.W. Bowen and Company: Indianapolis, Indiana, 1915

www.wesleymethodist.com/whoarewe/history

First Cumberland Presbyterian Church, 1844

First Cumberland Presbyterian Church, 1844, May 19
Division in 1849
New School congregation, 1849, April 23 (Old Calvary Church)
Old School congregation in 1860, August 28 (Calvary Presbyterian Church)
became First Presbyterian Church, 1906
merger of First Presbyterian and Calvary Presbyterian churches, 1930, July 10
First & Calvary Presbyterian Church

Much like the earlier Methodist congregations, the Presbyterians were early founders of church beginnings in Springfield. They, too, would be divided and greatly influenced by theology, church politics and the Civil War. In 1837, the Presbyterian Church in America developed a deep split, the Old School and New School. The Old School had a more conservative theology, did not support revivals, and called for traditional Calvinist orthodoxy. They were supported by the more traditional Scotch-Irish immigrants. The New School strongly favored revivalism, interdenominational cooperation (especially with the Congregationalists), and was a more Americanized product, especially in the westward expansion in the 1800s.

There were further divisions within each of the Schools because of more detailed theological differences and the Civil War. The Old School was initially in sympathy more with the Southern position on slavery and states' rights. The New School was more inclined to be in sympathy with the Union.

The Springfield Congregation of the Cumberland Presbyterian Church was organized in May 1844, through the efforts of C.B. Holland, a Union soldier from Tennessee now farming in Springfield. There were eighteen charter members and one "black woman." The group met on Sunday afternoons in the small Methodist Episcopal log cabin built in 1833. In 1859, the group began construction on their own building at the southwest corner of Jefferson Avenue and Olive Street. Even this small group became so divided over the issue of slavery that they ceased meeting just before and during the Civil War. The building remained unfinished.

The first edifice built and used by First Cumberland Presbyterian Church at the southwest corner of Jefferson and Olive. Begun in 1859 and completed ten years later, it served the congregation until it was razed in 1890.

The group, now known as the First Cumberland Presbyterian Church, reorganized in 1868. Ten years later, the earlier unfinished church building was completed with a capacity to seat four hundred people. The church flourished in the 1870s, even hosting the General Assembly of the Cumberland Presbyterian Church for the first time. A new building was needed and the construction plans began in 1890. The old building was razed and during construction, services were held in the YMCA at the corner of Campbell Avenue and College Street. The new building was dedicated in 1892 at the same site on Jefferson Avenue and Olive Street. Membership grew throughout the 1890s reaching nearly three hundred.

By 1902, membership had climbed to three hundred and seventy-two. That same year, the church again hosted the General Assembly of the Cumberland Presbyterian Church. But in 1906, with some apparent resolve of the past differences, the congregation voted to unite with the Presbyterian Church, (USA). The church's name was changed to the First Presbyterian Church, (USA). A few of the members dissented and remained committed to the Cumberland Presbyterian cause. They met in a store building for a while until a building could be used for the group at the southwest corner of Broadway Avenue and Division Street. Through a generous donation in 1921, the congregation moved to the new basement location at the northeast corner of Grand Street and Clay Avenue. A sanctuary was built over the basement in 1927. During the forty years at this site, the church experienced several periods of con-

First Cumberland Presbyterian Church, 2017

flict with the pastoral leadership. In 1959, the church, for the third time, hosted the General Assembly of the Cumberland Presbyterian Church.

In 1970, the church again rebuilt at a new location, the southeast corner of South Charleston Avenue and Republic Road, their current location. On May 19, 1994, they celebrated their 150th anniversary.

Current Information

4216 S. Charleston Ave., Springfield, MO 65804
(417) 883-4248
www.firstcp.net

Resources Used

Fare, Michael. *The Unifinished Story of First Cumberland Presbyterian Church.* One Hundred and Fiftieth Anniversay, May 19, 1994

Meyer, Duane and Arnold, V. Marie. *A Brief History of First and Calvary Presbyerian Church, Springfield, Missouri.* 1987

Stringfield, E.E. *Presbyterianism in the Ozarks, 1834-1907.* 1909

"Who Are the Cumberland Presbyterians?" pamphlet, Cumberland Presbyterian Resources, Item #557-706

www.en.ikipedia.org/wiki/Cumberland_Presbyterian_Church

www.firstcp.net/

www.presbyterianmission.org/ministries/101/history/"

www.the library.org/lochist/history/paspres/hollandc.html

www.wikipedia.org/wiki/Presbyterian_ Church_(U.S.A.)

www.wikipedia.org/wiki/Old_School%E2%80%93New_School_Controversy

Calvary Presbyterian Church, 1849

The roots of Calvary Presbyterian Church are found in the early beginning of the Cumberland Presbyterian Church. The division of the Old and New Schools and the Civil War found a collection of Cumberland members favoring the Old School and the Southern position on slavery. A collection of New School Presbyterian Springfield residents and area locals established the Presbyterian Church of Springfield on April 23, 1849. The fourteen members called Reverend Daniel Emmerson on August 12, 1849. One year later he was dismissed because of tensions arising over perceived feeling of his pro-abolitionist sentiments. For a while the name of the Presbytery was dropped until after 1860. Meeting places varied from the School House, the Court House, the residence of David Appleby, the Little Prairies School House, Hall's School House and the Methodist Church. On July 4, 1858, construction of their own building was completed between East Walnut and East Elm Streets. Division grew within the church regarding positions of the Old and New Schools. The groups began to meet alternately in the building with the Old School calling its own pastor, Reverend James A. Quarles. On August 28, 1860, the Old School group established its own church, named "Calvary Presybterian Church of Springfield." Other Old Schoolers in the area joined the group of now 31 members.

The Civil War not only brought further division, but also the loss of the building. It was sold for debt by order of the civil court. A member of the Calvary Presbyterian (Old School) group was able to purchase the building and would have legal claim after the war ended. After the battle of Wilson's Creek on August 10, 1861, every church facility in Springfield was used as a hospital or storehouse for military armaments. The Old and New School groups, aided by Union victory and local control, found some spiritual relief under the leadership of Union Post Chaplain Wines, who held several community worship services and Sunday School classes.

The first installed pastor of the church, after the war ended in April 1865, was Reverend James A. Paige. He and his family came from St. Louis and he was installed February 14, 1867. With returning troops, families and a large number of war immigrants, the community and the church began a period of significant growth. Springfield, now having grown to over 5,500 in population, saw the arrival of a railroad line and the first public school system. The church became financially independent in 1869.

Old Calvary Church

Meetings for the church as well as regional gatherings found the building facilties woefully inadequate. In 1870, construction was begun on a new church building at the corner of St. Louis Street and Benton Avenue. In 1872, the largest revival ever held in Springfield was at Calvary Presbyterian Church. It required the use of the Mansfield Opera House on South Street. The church grew in membership to 239. The new church building was completed in 1879.

The decade of the 1880s found the church reaching out to the community to establish new churches. 1n 1883, thirteen members helped organize the Central Congregational Church (which later established Drury College, later Drury University). In 1885, twenty-two members helped establish the Second Presbyterian Church at North Benton Avenue and Locust Street. The church would be dissolved years later. That same year, thirty-one members helped establish Westminster Presbyterian Church, later located at the corner of Cherry Street and National Avenue. At the turn of the century, new mission works were started in the city. A mission, known as Fairmont Chapel, was also started on St. Louis Street just east of National Avenue. Another mission would be started in the building of the Swedish Church on the north side of Chestnut Street between Boonville and Robberson Avenues. It became known as the Leard Chapel.

The church continued its growth and outreach through a series of committed and talented pastors and church leaders through the early decades of the 1900s. The church growth required a serious evaluation

First and Calvary Church

of the inadequate and deteriorating old building. The financial crash of 1929 ruled out the possibility of constructing a bigger facility. At the same time, the First Presbyterian Church had just completed its new building at the corner of Cherry Street and Dollison Avenue. It was now deeply in debt. Discussions were held about merging the two congregations. It was readily agreed to by a majority of both churches. On July 10, 1930, Calvary Presbyterian Church voted 227 to 176 to merge with First Presbyterian Church, effective October 1. The first worship service of the First and Calvary Presbyterian Church was held on October 5, 1930.

Resources Used

Meyer, Duane and Arnold, V. Marie. *A Brief History of First and Calvary Presbyterian Church, Springfield, Missouri.* 1987

Old Calvary Church, 1849-1949, centennial booklet

First Presbyterian Church, 1860

First Presbyterian Church, ca. 1980s

The history of the First Presbyterian Church is tied directly to the history of the Cumberland Presbyterian Church in Springfield. It created its separate identity in 1906 with the union of the Presbyterian Church (USA). The church's name was changed to the First Presbyterian Church (USA). A few of the members dissented and remained committed to the Cumberland Presbyterian cause.

The church was comparitively large in membership, with 675 members by 1914. The church building at Jefferson Avenue and Olive Street was soon overshadowed by much larger, adjacent business buildings. The building dating back to 1882 was in need of major repairs. It was recorded in a history of Greene County at the time:

> *It will not be surprising if the growing encroachments of business, with its bustle and noise, already pressing closely upon it, shall make advisable at no distant day the sale of the present property and the erection of a new and more commodious house of worship at a spot not too far removed from the city's active life, while ministering also to the contemplative side of Christian worship.*

After a search for a new location, the site at Cherry Street and Dollison Avenue was selected for the new building. The land was purschased on November 4, 1928. Construction began on June 2, 1929, and the dedication was held on February 16, 1930.

With the new construction debt incurred at the time of the financial crash in late 1929, the church needed financial help through increased giving and an increased membership. The solution came in the possible merger with the Calvary Presbyterian Church. On July 10, 1930,

First and Calvary Church

the church voted 257 to 59 to merge with Calvary Presbyterian Church. Significant opposition among the minority votes led to a meeting of the Presbytery and after fierce discussion on both sides, the eighteen delegates unaninmously approved the merger on October 1, 1930. The name was changed to First and Calvary Presbyterian Church.

Resources Used

Meyer, Duane and Arnold, V. Marie. *A Brief History of First and Calvary Presbyterian Church, Springfield, Missouri.* 1987

Old First Church, 1844-1944, centennial booklet

First and Calvary Presbyterian Church, 1930

First and Calvary Presbyterian Church, 1952

After the merger of the two congreagtions in 1930, the church was fortunate to have leadership from a series of strong and effective pastors. Dr. Arthur J. McClung served as pastor from 1930-1962. His very able administrative leadership provided confidence in the merger and helped to eliminate the church indebtedness by 1946. A much needed educational wing was able to be added in 1952.

Dr. William E. Everheart served as pastor from 1962-1971. His ministry led the church to be more involved in the community and improved the inner workings of the church. The Sunday worship was broadcast to the community, women were elected to be elders and deacons (1963) and the church became deeply involved in the Council of Churches. Much needed parking space was added with the paving of

First and Calvary Presbyterian Church, 1980

First and Calvary Presbyterian Church

Memorial Park across from the church on Dollison Street. Dr. Everheart was selected as the president of local Drury College in 1971.

Dr. Jack Hart served as pastor beginning in 1972. The church continued and expanded its ministry in the Council of Churches. The ministry of Crosslines was housed in the church. A nearby house was purchased by the church and used as a women's shelter. An increased interest and participation by the church in international ministries began. A program of summer projects was begun for students helping in local ministry needs. Two major facility improvements during his ministry were the purchase of a new organ and a new circle drive added in 1979.

The church experienced significant growth during this period when other downtown churches were in decline. Even with the growth, the church began facing a financial shortfall during the economic recession of the early 1980s. After painful but necessary staff cuts, the church was able to stay within a feasible budget. The situation caused the church to renew its financial commitments and improve later budgets.

Current Information

820 East Cherry Street, Springfield, MO 65806
(417) 862-5068
www.firstandcalvary.org/content.cfm?id=521

Resources Used

Fairbanks, Jonathan and Tuck, Clyde Edwin, *Past and Present of Greene County, Missouri*, Chapter 19, Church Denomination History

Fare, Michael. *The Unifinished Story of First Cumberland Presbyterian Church.*

One Hundred and Fiftieth Anniversary, May 19, 1994

First & Calvary Centennial, 1849-1949 booklet, pages 14-17

Meyer, Duane and Arnold, V. Marie. *A Brief History of First and Calvary Presbyterian Church, Springfield, Missouri.* 1987

Stringfield, E.E. *Presbyterianism in the Ozarks, 1834-1907.* 1909

www.firstandcalvary.org/content.cfm?id=521

www.presbyterianmission.org/ministries/101/history/

www.thelibrary.org/lochist/postcards/calvary_presbyterian.cfm

www.wikipedia.org/wiki/Cumberland_Presbyterian_Church

www.wikipedia.org/wiki/Presbyterian_ Church_(U.S.A.)

www.wikipedia.org/wiki/Old_School%E2%80%93New_School_ Controversy

First and Calvary Presbyterian Church, 2017

Wilson's Creek Chapel, 1847 Pitts Chapel United Methodist Church, 1911

Before 1847, slaves met secretly for worship in the woods around Wilson's Creek, also known as Jordan Creek. A slave petitioned his owner, William Townsend, to allow the slaves who were worshipping there to build a log cabin on the banks of Wilson's (Jordan) Creek. They would wait until October 31, 1847, when the mayor of Springfield granted to slave Tom (Townsend) Armstrong, permission for the organization of "colored people" within the Methodist Episcopal faith to have a class. With their log cabin completed, they met there and in various places throughout the city before and during the Civil War. Not all slave owners were happy with the arrangements, as other slaves joined with them without their owners' permission.

In 1863, Reverend Edgar Pitts became pastor and served three different times in that role. Reverend Pitts was a leader in the black community of Springfield, known by some as "Happy Hollow" and "Black Harlem." The congregation erected a frame building on Water Street, a little east of Benton Avenue. Reverend Pitts was a delegate, in 1870, to the Republican county convention. That same year, black men voted for the first time. They continued in this church structure until 1873, when a new brick building was constructed at the northeast corner of Jefferson Avenue and Water Street. Reverend Pitts died in 1899. Twelve years later, the church would be renamed in his honor. The Central Missouri Conference met in Pitts Chapel March 26, 1890.

Prejudice and lawlessness were still very present in Springfield. One of the saddest examples occurred in April 1906, when a mob of 5,000 witnessed the lynching of three black men on the electric tower on the public square. Two of the men were members of Pitts Chapel. The three were later found innocent of the charges of sexual assault and no one was ever declared guilty of the horrendous crime. However, the event terrified the black community and an immediate exodus of black residents occurred. This decreased membership and activity in the black churches of Springfield.

Pitts Chapel United Methodist Church

Church growth was also limited by the location near a sidetrack of the Frisco railway. Surrounding businesses also limited the capacity to expand the facility. Despite the distractions, the church continued its regular meetings and ministries. The church continued to search for a more favorable site, and, finally, a location was found at the northeast corner of Benton Avenue and Pine Street. The old building was demolished and the property sold. A new, larger brick structure was dedicated September 20, 1912, and renamed Pitts Chapel.

Under the direction of the pastor, Reverend J.M. Harris, D.D., the church now experienced a period of solid growth, with a Sunday School enrollment of 98. At the twenty-ninth annual session of the Central Missouri Conference in 1915, the church reported 326 members.

The church has been noted for its nurturing and training of future church leaders who were prominent in the history of the United Methodist Church. It has also found within its membership patriotic leaders active in the armed services of the United States. One such member was William Canafax. He was born in Greene County February 9, 1885. He volunteered for military service in October 1905, joining Company H, 301st Infantry as a supply sergeant. He saw action in the Spanish-American War and World War I in France. A later descendant and church member, Jackson Canafax would write:

Many sainted souls through the years have led prayer and class meetings to make Springfield a better place to rear their children. They kept the fires burning on the altar of prayer for guidance because they knew that without the way there is no going; without the truth there is no knowing; without the life there is no living.

May we say to you, the living, that the character of those you follow has left a high standard. We should not let them down. From generation to generation the church is rising upward toward its perfection, and though one after another of the workmen pass away, the great task remains and the great master builder carries on the undertaking. It is our task to build our portion on a solid and substantial manner, that they who follow us may be thankful for our thoroughness and inspired by our examples. Remember—our Christianity is just a mere shadow unless we reflect Him who, being incarnate God, was incarnate goodness.

Another notable feature of Pitts Chapel was its amazing music ministry. The choirs were of such excellent quality and spirit that they were often asked to provide the music for annual conferences. One of the more outstanding choirs was under the leadership of Robert Wendell Duncan. In 1946, he organized the Young and Adult Choir of Pitts Chapel. He continued to lead them for over forty years of service and ministry as they performed across the nation. Other ministry and educational organizations of the church were organized and still serve today.

In 1954, the church underwent an extensive redecorating project. Family memorials and other donated gifts provided funds for the projects.

The Springfield community also played an important role in the ongoing history of Pitts Chapel. In the 1960s, Mr. and Mrs. Lester Cox became involved with the church, providing financial support and leadership. Mrs. Cox also served for a while as secretary. When the physical facilities were in need of major repairs, volunteers from Schweitzer Methodist Church offered many hours of assistance, as well as financial support. The nearby Jordan Valley Community Center also provided financial assitance.

The church became affiliated, in 1968, with the newly-organized United Methodist Church. The church is recognized as one of the state's historical landmarks and is seeking application for the national registry.

Pitts Chapel United Methodist Church, 2017

Current Information

600 North Benton Avenue (417) 866-1720
www.facebook.com/pages/Pitts-Chapel-United-Methodist-Church

Resources Used

Black Families of the Ozarks, Volumes One and Two. Greene County Archives Bulletin Number Forty-Five, 2001.

Fairbanks, Jonathan and Tuck, Clyde Edwin. *Past and Present of Greene County Missouri, Volume 1*, A.W. Bowen and Company: Indianapolis, Indiana, 1915, pages 23-24

Greene County Clerk's Office

History of Pitts Chapel United Methodist Church, Beginning 1847, Springfield, Missouri, 1985, Historical and Records Committee, Margaret Canafax O'Neal, Chairperson

Recorded minutes from Pitts Chapel archives *Tops Journal*, "Your Neighbor's Faith," Katherine Lederer, January, 1983

www.facebook.com/pages/Pitts-Chapel-United-Methodist-Church

www.manta.com/c/mmyvrbj/pitts-chapel-united-methodist

www.moumethodist.org/churchdetails/697676

First Baptist Church, 1852

In the early summer months of 1852, Reverend B. McCord Roberts and eleven others met in a small brick house on Olive Street and organized the First Baptist Church of Springfield, Missouri. This organizational meeting was the result of years of prayer and faithful work by the early settlers from Tennessee and Kentucky.

The earliest known work of Baptists in the southwest Missouri area was, again, work of itinerant, circuit riding preachers. Reverend Braxton McCord Roberts led the outreach work of two earlier established churches in Greene County: Mt. Pleasant and Liberty. These churches and five new churches (with 112 members) established the Liberty Baptist Association in 1840, which conducted business sessions and sponsored summer camp meeting revival services. Church membership grew as a result of these efforts. In his circuit riding experiences, Reverend Roberts became aware of a few Baptist residents in Springfield expressing a need for a local church within the city. He shared those concerns with the Liberty Baptist Church. In July 1851, the church voted to support such a work and "any member of this church who wishes to join the branch at Springfield in answer to a petition of some of the brethren of that place." Nine of the original eleven meeting for the organization of the First Baptist Church were members of the Liberty Baptist Church.

This faithful group of believers would meet in various houses and facilities available within the city. The congregation grew and with their limited income worked together to construct their first church building near South and Elm Streets. On January 3, 1861, they began to use their new building. They would enjoy the new facility for only a few months. In June, 1861, the church building was seized by the Union military forces. The seizure of the building, and the ravages and divisions of the Civil War, found the small congregation unable to meet for five years. This was the common fate at that time for other churches and public buildings in Springfield. Some sources indicate that only a Presbyterian church held regular services in Springfield during the Civil War period.

A small group of thirteen members were gathered in 1866 to reorganize the First Baptist Church. In the reconstruction era, ministers were required to take an "ironclad oath" that they never supported the South. A series of short-term ministers led the church to make significant growth, and within a year, the congregation had grown to 168 members. They regained their early building in 1868, and began remodeling efforts. Under more stable and longer-term pastorates, remodeling efforts carried on through 1882, when a tower and additional rooms were added. The sanctuary could seat 300 people. The building was also used by black Baptists.

A hallmark of this growing congregation was that it began a history of establishing new church work in the community. A mission effort was begun in 1883 on East Commercial Street in then, North Springfield. Two years later, on March 1, 1885, the North Springfield Baptist Church was formally organized. The church would be renamed twice: in 1905, it was called the Robberson Avenue Church; in 1945, it was called the Second Baptist Church. The church rapidly became self-sufficient financially and experienced steady growth.

A second mission effort began in January 1891, with a Sunday School meeting at the Boulevard Hotel. By August, sufficient growth allowed for the purchase of nearby land and construction of a building. The Boulevard Baptist Church was organized that same year, but returned to mission status until 1912, with the name changing to the Pythian Avenue Baptist Church. In 2016, the church changed its name again to the Just for Jesus Church.

A third mission effort was established in 1891 becoming the Grant Avenue Baptist Church. It also returned to mission status until 1905. It is noted that the nation suffered from severe financial crises during the late 1880s and early 1890s. This accounted for the difficulties of these mission efforts to gain self sufficiency. The First Baptist Church continued financial support of these mission efforts during that period.

Even with the financial obligation of supporting two mission programs, First Baptist Church was able to finance construction of a new worship and education facility in 1895. The strong growth of Springfield's population, along with the evangelistic spirit of the church saw dramatic increase in membership. From 213 members in 1899, there was a five-fold increase to 1,104 members by 1915. This required an increase in organization and facilities. New staff positions were created and educational space was added in 1917.

In spite of the disruptions of World War I, the upcoming stock market crash of 1929, the prolonged Depression of the 1930s, and growing international unrest, First Baptist Church maintained its primary purposes with strong economic support. A building fund was established in 1928, for a new church and education space. In addition, two new mission sites were begun. In 1927, the College Street Baptist Church was organized with a building and strong work. Another mission effort began in 1929 with the Southwest Baptist Mission. The Southwest Baptist Church was organized later that year. It would change its name in 1931, to the Tabernacle Baptist Church. In 1939, the name would change again to the Temple Baptist Church.

The continued growth of the building fund and the plans for new construction were put on hold with the United States entry into World War II. The pastor even enlisted in the Navy as a chaplain. During the war years, unrest began to take shape within the church membership. Even with a new pastor, there were personality conflicts and open dissention over church policies. A smoldering dissention developed into open rebellion. Dual alliances with the Northern and Southern Baptist Conventions were challenged. In November 1945, sixty-five members asked and received letters of dismissal from First Baptist Church. They organized the University Heights Baptist Church retaining the dual alignment. The departures created a brief decline in the church attendance and financial support.

The postwar years saw a national period of growth and expansion. Springfield also shared in that experience. Businesses, schools and

First Baptist Church, 1957

First Baptist Church, 1980s

churches experienced significant growth. First Baptist Church pushed for a big building fund increase and finally voted to build the new church. The first services were held on September 9, 1951.

A new four-story education building, named after Pastor Fred Eastham, was constructed in 1956. Another mission support was begun by the church and in 1961, it was organized into the Homeland Baptist Church. That same year, the church began to publish a new weekly newsletter, *The Messenger*. The decade of the 1960s was a high mark for the growth of First Baptist Church's organizations, membership and outreach, all under the very capable leadership of Pastor Thomas Field. The church membership exceeded 3,000 during his ministry. It was also a time of international and national unrest with military involvement in Southeast Asia, political assassinations (national and international), and political distrust. As with nearly every community in the nation, Springfield felt the impact in its schools and churches.

First Baptist Church had nearly always benefited from long pastorates. Such would be the case with Pastor Thomas T. Crabtree. He served as pastor from 1971 until 1990. A new activities education building was dedicated for use on September 7, 1975. An expanding youth and children's program benefited directly from the new facility. The church was now viewed as the leading church in Missouri and recognized as a leading church in supporting Southern Baptist mission causes. The church celebrated its 125th anniversary in June 1977.

In 1979, the Southern Baptist Convention saw an effort to take over the convention through a series of actions designed to control the nominating process and eventual control of convention boards.

First Baptist Church, 1984

Successful rightwing, political tactics were employed with a successful, fundamentalist takeover completed within just a few years. There were tragic impacts on state conventions, associations and larger churches. The Missouri Baptist Convention experienced a similar fundamentalist takeover by the 1990s and churches in the state were forced to take sides. Traditional Baptists ousted by the new convention leadership formed new national Baptist organizations, such as the Cooperative Baptist Fellowship (CBF). First Baptist Church in Springfield was caught in this web of denominational strife. Dr. Crabtree had become very disturbed by the convention events before his retirement.

Beginning in 1991, a series of much shorter-term pastorates faced the challenge of denominational battles in the convention and internal power battles within the church. A strong minority in the church favored the CBF and gave their financial support through First Baptist Church, Springfield. Groups polarized in the church continued to press for control and church identity. Some were dissatisfied with continuing to support Southern Baptist Convention programs. Others were intent on not allowing any gifts to the CBF to be made through the church. Other side issues came into play, such as the ordination of women as deacons. In March 1997, things came to head after a series of secret meetings and very uncivilized, public meetings. The group favoring the CBF had been ostracized from all church life. Over 200

First Baptist Church, 2017

members left First Baptist Church Springfield, with 100 going to University Heights Baptist Church and the other 100 going to other places. [The religion editor for the *Springfield News-Leader* had observed early on that the conflict was inaccurately labeled as the fundamentalists versus the moderates. It was more correctly a battle between the intolerants and the tolerants.]

With the church now completely committed to First Baptist Church causes, there was need to recover from the membership and financial losses. It was also a time to seek a new pastor and get back to basic purposes of the church. The church also began to prepare for the 150th anniversary of the church to be celebrated in June 2002.

Although the church record reflects periods of dissension and turmoil, the total record reflects much to be praised. The largest church in Springfield unselfishly began numerous missions and new church starts. In its history, the church has started seven missions in the city with five of those now being strong self-supporting churches. The membership gave sacrificially to finance these new starts, as well as construction of new facilities. The church has always maintained a strong evangelistic fervor for the local community. The church was fortunate to have been led by some of the best leadership in Baptist circles.

Current Information

525 South Avenue, Springfield, MO 65806
(417) 866-7202
www.fbcspringfield.com/

Resources Used

A History of the First Baptist Church, Springfield, Missouri, 1852–1977, by Wayne C. Bartee

An Unofficial History of the First Baptist Church of Springfield, Missouri, 1978-2002, by Wayne C. Bartee

Fairbanks, Jonathan and Tuck, Clyde Edwin. *Past and Present of Greene County Missouri, Volume 1*, A.W. Bowen and Company: Indianapolis, Indiana, 1915

First Baptist Church, Springfield, Missouri, 100th Anniversary Program, June 9, 1852–June 9, 1952

www.fbcspringfield.com

Christ (Protestant) Episcopal Church, 1859

Unlike the early Methodist and Presbyterian churches in Springfield, First Baptist and Christ Episcopal remained comparatively united in their early history. The first meeting of the Christ Episcopal Parish was in 1859 in the Calvary Presbyterian Church. As with the other churches in Springfield, the Civil War interrupted regular services. Occasional meetings took place as military chaplains led community worship services. Following the war, in 1866, the members built a small church on Walnut Street, between Campbell Avenue and Market Street. It measured 25' x 25', seated fifty worshippers and was on leased land. On April 12, 1868, lightning struck the church during Sunday School and damaged a significant part of the south end of the building. Major fundraising activities began through the women's organization and a new site was purchased on the corner of east Walnut Street and Kimbrough Avenue.

In addition to the funds raised, a loan was secured to build the new church building. Frustrations also developed over funding for the rector salary. Again, a loan was secured for temporary salary payment. The first service in the new facility was on New Year's Eve, 1870. A church could not be consecrated with an existing debt. Finally, March

Christ Episcopal Church

8, 1872, a consecration worship service was held. It was nearly a decade later before adequate heating would be installed and needed repairs made on the church front. The building was described as a "Medieval style, with English belfry, an imitation of Gothic architecture." It is the oldest sanctuary still in use in Springfield.

In the 1880s, nearby properties were purchased for investment purposes. A new work was begun in north Springfield which later developed into the St. John's Episcopal Church. The following decade would see a new rectory built and major internal improvements made.

Several times in the early 1900s, the church considered moving to a new location and building a larger facility. Each time the decision was to remain where they were and expand. Reasons for the decision were the high cost of building and strong sentimental and historical ties to the present location. In the 1920s, when major repairs were once again needed, the church decided to repair and expand. A new chancel and school building was completed with debt that remained until after the Depression era.

In 1933, Dr. Sears Riepma began his service as rector. In his memoirs written years later, he recalled the situation he found at the church:

> *In the early Depression years, parishes found it increasingly difficult to maintain themselves especially after many years of free spending and accumulated indebtedness. Christ Church in Springfield, Missouri had not been laggard in that matter during the roaring twenties. They had built a parish house and a new chancel of stone, intending to have future financial obligations covered by some of the insurance. That plan had fallen through and while the building went on, money being raised for it faltered. It was easier to borrow the money from a bank... and the poor parish floated on a sea of debt... the Bishop saw correctly that the parish either had to close or be reduced to mission status.*

Dr. Riepma led the church through the very difficult financial challenge and did much of the internal building improvements himself. Aesthetic improvements were made to the interior of the parish hall. He began a popular radio ministry in 1934 over KWTO radio that lasted for over thirty years. During his ministry, the church actually increased in membership. By 1948, there were over 833 communicants. Improvements on the church grounds were made. He served the church faithfully until his retirement in 1950.

Christ Episcopal Church

The 1950s, saw a new rectory built as well as additional education space. This was done with the membership raising and exceeding the needed funds. Necessary replacements were made for electrical and heating systems. Other improvements were added in the new education space.

In the 1960s, the church dealt with local, racial issues, burned the parish hall mortgage note, paved the parking lot, received nearby donated properites for future growth and contributed to emergency needs of local youth organizations. The new rector was also very involved in community affairs. He was chaplain at the Medical Center for Federal Prisoners for fifteen years and served as chaplain for the Springfield

Christ Episcopal Church after its renovation in 2007

Christ Episcopal Church, 2017

Police Department. The church continued to be blessed with continued donations and memorial gifts that allowed the decade to end with the elimination of all church indebtedness and a sizable financial balance available for use.

Air conditioning was added in the early 1970s, and several important memorial funds were left for specific ministries. The church was added to the official National Register of Historic Places in 1987. An extensive restoration of the building and site was made. The downtown location required a security system to be installed throughout the church in the 1990s. The church become involved with an outreach emphasis to ministries in Haiti.

In 2005, construction began on a new expanded parish hall and classroom space. While construction was underway, the church was able to use the facilities of Grace Methodist Church. The construction projects were completed in 2007.

Current Information

601 East Walnut Street, Springfield, MO 65806
(417) 866-5133
www.ChristEpiscopalChurch.com

Resources Used

Christ Episcopal Church, Serving Our Savior for 150 Years, GPH, Springfield, MO, 2009

Fairbanks, Jonathan and Tuck, Clyde Edwin. *Past and Present of Greene County Missouri, Volume 1*, A.W. Bowen and Company: Indianapolis, Indiana, 1915

www.christepiscopalchurch.diowestmo.org/history-of-christ-episcopal church.html

www.associations.missouristate.edu/trails/historic_churches_in_springfield.html

Chapter Two

1860s

Historical Notes

The dominant historical event of the early 1860s, was the Civil War. The conflict had significant impact on the nation, within states and especially on key cities. Springfield was no exception. The second great battle fought in Civil War occurred a few miles southwest of Springfield at Wilson's Creek. Union forces gathered in Springfield, traveled to Wilson's Creek, fought a Confederate force in a horrendous battle with numerous losses on both sides. Following the battle, probably decided as a draw, the Union forces retreated to Springfield to regroup and care for the wounded. Local schoolhouses and church buildings had been confiscated by the military for billeting, storage and recovery. For several years following, the city seesawed between control of Union and Confederate forces. Finally, in 1863, the Confederate forces left the city in Union hands until the end of the war.

As in many other communities, the Civil War created divisions of loyalty. Missouri felt the divisions perhaps the strongest of any of the states. As a compromise state over the slavery issue, many of the Springfield residents had family roots in the South and many owned slaves. The divisions of loyalty not only affected families and neighbors, but also affected the churches. Many of the churches ceased meeting altogether and eventually created new churches which expressed their common loyalties.

At the end of the Civil War in 1865, the city population had grown to 5,000. War-damaged buildings were repaired and the construction of new buildings increased with the arrival of the first railroad. On January 11, 1865, Missouri became the first slave state to emancipate its slaves before the adoption of the 13th Amendment of the U.S. Constitution. In July 1865, the city became part of wild west history. A famous shootout occurred on the town square between "Wild Bill"

Hickok and Davis Tutt. The incident and death of Davis Tutt made national news.

In 1867, a school board was elected and public school classes started. There were now ten churches in the city: Methodist, Methodist Episcopal South, Presbyterian, Cumberland Presbyterian, Baptist, Episcopal, Christian (Disciples), Catholic, "Colored" Methodist, and "Colored" Baptist.

The age of Reconstruction was a difficult time in Springfield, Missouri. Radicals were required to pledge allegiances to the Union so properties would not be confiscated. The realities of the great human losses for families created an atmosphere of despair, distrust and suspicion. The churches, being reorganized and remodeled, would provide some comfort and hope for the future.

Churches Established No Longer Qualifying

Union Evangelical (Congregational) Church, 1869

The name was changed in 1870 to the First Congregational Church. On May 21, 1872, they built a house of worship at the northeast corner of Jefferson Avenue and Locust Street. The church was active in establishing Drury College in 1873. Some members left in 1883, to establish the Central Congregational Church at the southeast corner of Walnut and Market Streets. It was disbanded in 1899. In 1901, a new church was built at the northeast corner of Calhoun Street and Benton Avenue. Financial difficulties caused the First Congregational Church to temporarily disband in 1908. A new effort to rebuild came in 1915, with the buildings being debt free. Their long association with Drury College continued for many years. The church building burned down in 1952.

Churches Currently Operating

- **Gibson Chapel Presbyterian Church**, 1865
- Second Baptist Church, 1867
  - Washington Avenue Baptist Church, 1904
  - **Turning Point**, 2016
- Tatum Chapel, 1867
  - **Freedom Baptist Church**, 1908
- **Immaculate Conception Catholic Church,** 1868

Gibson Chapel Presbyterian Church, 1865

At Washington and Tampa Streets in Springfield, Missouri, sits a red painted brick church. It houses the proud, strong heart of a black Presbyterian congregation, which celebrated their church's 150th birthday in May of 2016. Very little history of this church is published, and then only in snatches, which are at times conflicting. Several fires of undetermined origin destroyed all of the records of the church along with the stained glass windows, which once graced the building. Word of mouth from member to member and generation to generation keeps the history of the church alive.

The founders of this church started life as slaves, and those attending services were also in bondage. Faith in God was all they could call their own, and even as they met to celebrate that faith, their meetings were monitored. Slave preachers were suspected of encouraging rebellion and their preaching was, by law, to be monitored by white men. It is, however, thankfully reported that the law was seldom enforced. Coming out of slavery, they took great comfort in their freedom and their faith in God. The path wasn't easy as they began to educate themselves and strive to fit into the white world, even as Jim Crow laws were created to suppress them. Black churches in the community became ever more precious, comforting, and important as gathering places after emancipation.

One reference states that a constitution for a new Cumberland Presbyterian congregation was signed in Springfield in 1844, and one of the signers was said to be a black woman by the name of "Leah." No other reference to this woman or any other signers was found. At this time, a search found no documented evidence that the signing of this constitution had any significance to Gibson Chapel; as this date was well before the 1865 date associated with Peter Lear's arrival in Springfield. (The spelling of his last name was reported as changed from Lair. The Lair name was taken when Peter and his mother, both slaves, were sold or transferred by a family by the name of Weaver to the family named Lair.)

An individual by the name of Simon Headly is credited with the organization of the church, but his contributions appear to be question-

First location of Gibson Chapel, 1865

able. No data can be found to verify his connection to the church or any other reference that places him in Springfield. The date associated with Simon Headly is not until 1872.

No exact date of organization for Gibson Chapel is found, but it is acknowledged and accepted that 1865 is the year it had its beginning. It started as the Cumberland Presbyterian Church under the leadership of Peter Lear. The congregation met in a frame building "across the branch" (This refers to the Jordan Creek, which was paved over in 1884, beneath Water Street. The creek at this location was considered by the town fathers to be a nuisance due to frequent flooding.) This branch of the Jordan creek was by the Memphis Railroad tracks at the foot of Washington Avenue. The building was at the corners of Phelps Street and Jefferson Avenue and was shared with a Baptist church.

In a Springfield city directory of 1873, there is reference to a Cumberland Presbyterian Church (colored) at Water Street, between Benton and Washington Avenues. It is the first directory produced by the city, and the introduction states that it may contain errors and omissions due to difficulty collecting data. The location of the Cumberland Presbyterian Church listed is different than where the church was believed to be, but is within the same general area of the city. In the directory, the pastor of the church is listed as Robert Johnson and one of the elders is listed as William Gatewood, who is known to have donated the land where the current church is located. Another reference states that in 1872, Washington Avenue Baptist Church (colored) worshipped in a building in conjunction or with the Cumberland Presbyterians. The Washington Avenue Church built another church building in 1884, and the Presbyterians bought their interest in the building.

After the Civil War and emancipation, most of the blacks in Springfield lived close to the area around Jordan Creek and the railroad tracks in an area known as "Happy Hollow."

Through research there are two references to Peter Lear's birth. The first is from the family Bible of a Major Weaver who owned Peter, his mother and his siblings. Peter's mother's name is listed as Sitty in one reference and Letty in another. (Possibly the deciphering of handwriting could account for these differences in the records.) Peter's mother is recalled as a much beloved servant. The account in Major Weaver's family Bible lists her as having seven children. Peter's birthday in the Weaver Bible is said to be July 14, 1827, while reference from the Lair family places his birthdate as 1830. Peter Lear lived with the Lair family (from whom he took his name) until he was emancipated and freed and came to Springfield. It is said that he chose preaching as his profession at the age of eighteen and he was much sought after for his sermons. He preached and taught school in Springfield where he resided with his wife, Fanny Carson, also a freed slave. He purchased three acres of land on St. Louis Street in Springfield in 1866, and lived there for seventeen years. The couple was not known to have children of their own but were said to have adopted several. He was known as Father Lear to his congregation, which he led for many years. (There is contradiction in where Peter Lear and his wife Fanny Carson were living/and or freed…one reference points to Kentucky, while another states Dallas County, Texas.)

Rev. Gibson, namesake of Gibson Chapel Presbyterian Church

Other ministers, several of whom switched to the Methodist Church when Gibson Chapel left the Cumberland Presbytery, succeeded Peter Lear. Around this time is when the leadership passed to H.A. Gibson. An extensive search for information as to his background, such as time and place of birth and death, was unsuccessful. Gibson's popularity did much to enhance the growth of the church. It is recorded that he led a revival, which was responsible for the conversion of many who then joined the church. He served as the pastor for approximately 10 years, but did not live to see the construction of the new church building.

William Gatewood was a prominent businessman in Springfield when he donated the land where the church currently stands. Mr. Gatewood bought his and his wife's freedom from the McElhaney family in Fayetteville, Arkansas. He came to Springfield with Union Army General John Sanborn, who held command of the Department of Southwest Missouri during the Civil War.

Gibson Chapel as it looked in the early 20th century

The building of the new church began in 1891. It is a large, brick structure with a complete basement beneath and living quarters for the pastor in the rear. Tampa Street was, at the time, known as Pine Street. The cost was said to be in the range of $15,000.00. When money to pay for the church was needed, some in the congregation mortgaged their homes to raise the funds for construction. Some lost their homes because of this risk. The Gibson Chapel is a beautiful, fine building that was once the heart of a thriving neighborhood, but now the homes are

Members of Gibson Chapel Presbyterian Church, ca. 1940s.

gone and industry is Gibson's neighbor. The church took the name of the pastor they loved so well. When the church was complete, and as an act of symbolism, the congregation walked from their old church to "cross the Jordan as the Israelites' had crossed the Jordan to Jericho."

The church was one of the hubs of Springfield for blacks. The congregation, which numbered about 200 to 250, was comprised of people from all walks of life including the elite of the black community, teachers, business owners and the like; but also the servant workers in the city. Thursday was the servant's day off and some of the best cooks from private homes and the chefs from the fine restaurants gathered in the basement kitchen to cook for the congregation. The meals that were prepared are still the "talk of legends," and even today the church prepares and serves their famous fried chicken dinners several times a year.

This account would not be complete without including brief details of the hanging and burning of three falsely accused African American men. The circumstances of the event, which occurred in 1906, can be viewed in more detail in many references. It was a horror of uncontrolled mob violence when these men, Horace Duncan, Fred Coker and William Allen, were hung and their bodies burned after being falsely accused of robbery and rape. They were later declared innocent by a grand jury. This event had a profound effect on the congregation of Gibson Chapel. The congregants gathered at the church for protection, the women and children hiding in the basement while the men of the church kept watch with guns at the ready. The incident lasted several days and was not resolved until the National Guard was sent by the governor to restore order. The lynching had devastating consequences for the African American population. Many blacks left Springfield for good, and it is estimated that their numbers decreased by 50 percent.

A tornado that hit the Springfield area in January of 2008, did extensive damage to the chapel, flooding the basement and lifting the roof. The current pastor, Donald T. Glunt, said the tornado lifted the roof and put it back, but it did not sit as it once did. Now the interior of the church has a suspended ceiling to hide the extensive repairs. The congregation came together doing what they do best, cooking, to raise money to save their church. They sold food in a grassroots effort to help with the costly repairs to their church as no flood insurance was carried.

Gibson Chapel was saddened when it lost one of its favorite sons, Homer Boyd. Mr. Boyd and all the members of the famed Philharmonics singing group were members of Gibson Chapel. They had their start in the 1950s, with help from Florence Sample Thomas, wife of the pastor and the director of the choir. They made many appearances at the Grand Ole Opry television show and were regularly featured on the Ozark Jubilee, a television show filmed in Springfield. Mr. Boyd was a well-known figure in Springfield and made many contributions to the community. His death in June of 2016, was unexpected.

Gibson Chapel was received into the Presbyterian Church (USA) in the fall of 1914, and they remain with that organization to this day.

For the last twenty years, Pastor Donald Glunt has served the church congregation. His pride and love for this church shows and he considers it a privilege to call the congregation his family.

When Gibson celebrated their 150th birthday in May of 2016, the theme for the celebration was "Ringing Out Christ for 150 Years." They took that symbolic walk to cross the Jordan as part of their anniversary celebration, as had their ancestors before them. They had a successful weekend of remembering and fellowship. In the program for the event is a quote attributed to Dr. Martin Luther King: "Faith is taking the first step even when you don't see the whole staircase." This quote speaks volumes about what this church has endured and accomplished since their beginning. They continue to take the next step forward with determination, devotion to their faith, and their love of God.

Gibson Chapel Presbyterian Church, 2017

Current Information

536 East Tampa Street
(417) 865-1410
www.facebook.com/GibsonChapel

References

Digitalcollections.missouristate.edu/cem4/browse.php?CISOROOT=/LedererExhibit

Fairbanks, Jonathan and Tuck, Clyde Edwin, *Past and Present of Greene County Missouri*, thelibrary.org.

Greenecountymo.gov/archives/Springfield/sc1873/index.php (pages 9–25)

History of Laclede, Camden, Dallas, Webster, Wright, Texas, Pulaski, Phelps, And Dent Counties, Missouri. The Goodspeed Publishing Company, 1889, page 1182

Katherine G. Lederer Ozarks African American History Collection – library.missouristate.edu/archives/ /lederer.htm

Many Thousands Gone: Springfield's Lost Black History

Sketch 1873 Springfield City Directory – Greene County Home Page

www.facebook.com/GibsonChapel/

Second Baptist Church, 1867
Washington Avenue Baptist Church, 1904
Turning Point, 2016

We had hoped to include more information about this church. Yet, after repeated contact attempts, the church has not responded to our requests for information on their organizational history. We have found some limited information from secondary sources that we have included.

Second Baptist Church, 1892

The church was organized as the Second Baptist Church in 1867. They first met in a building on the southwest corner of the public square. With the assistance of the Cumberland Presbyterians, a frame building was erected, in 1872, at the corner of Benton Avenue and Water Street. They worshipped there for over ten years.

In 1884, a lot was purchased at 729 North Washington Avenue and a brick house for worship was built. An addition was added in 1892, and a cornerstone was laid. Rev. Steven Frost was the first pastor and Sister Lottie Freeman was one of the charter members.

In 1904, a new building of worship was constructed at the Washington Avenue site. The original cornerstone was placed upside down in the southwest corner of the new structure. It was laid by the grand master mason, D.W. Williams of Booneville, Missouri. Pastor J.S. Dorsey conducted the dedicatory service. In attendance were former pastors J.T. Carson, Cohren, Sawyer, and other outstanding ministers of that time. That year the church changed its name to refelct the new location. It was thought by some that the term "second" was demeaning for a black church and many were already referring to the church by its location.

Turning Point Church, formerly known as Washington Avenue Baptist Church, 2017

Church growth and outreach was interrupted on Thanksgiving morning, November 30, 1911. Fire destroyed the pews, windows, two organs and most of the pastor's library. The damage was cleared and the building was rebuilt soon after. Seventy years later, on February 9, 1984, another fire was started by an arsonist in the church annex.

A new building and location was completed without debt on October 8, 2000. The new home was located at 1722 North National Avenue. The old Washington Avenue church building was "restored, preserved and relocated" one block to the north by Drury University for use as a diversity center and the home of the Springfield Chapter of the NAACP.

On July 23, 2008, an old cornerstone for a "Second Baptist Church" was found under a hedge at 1639 North National Avenue. It was taken to the current Second Baptist Church on Battlefield Street. The date on the cornerstone was listed as 1885, long before the current Second Baptist Church adopted the name. After some research by Pastor John Marshall (a historian himself), he discovered the actual origin of the cornerstone and returned it to the Washington Avenue Church.

The site at National Avenue has been remodeled and updated with the addition of a paved parking lot. The current Pastor, Dr. Edward L. Alexander is leading the church to focus on the whole man to "Empower People to Live A Life of Victory." In 2016, the name was changed to Turning Point.

Current Information

1722 North National Avenue
(417) 866-2750
www.washingtonavechurch.org

Resources Used

www.washingtonavechurch.org/Ministry-Services-About-US-Springfield-MO.html Fairbanks and Tuck, *Past and Present of Greene County, Missouri*, 1915

Tatum Chapel, 1867
Freedom Baptist Church, 1908

We had hoped to include more information about this church. Yet, after repeated contact attempts, the church has not responded to our requests for information on their organizational history. We have found some limited information from secondary sources that we have included.

Tatum Chapel was organized with fourteen members in February 1867. Under the pastoral leadership of Rev. G.W. White (a former pastor of the First Baptist Church, Springfield), the group held services in a local log cabin. The group met one Sunday a month. Land for a church building was donated by Brian Tatum. After a church building was completed, the church outgrew its facilities. A larger church building was erected after 1909. Over the next two decades, improvements were made to the facilities with electric lights replacing gasoline lanterns and a floor furnace replacing the pot-bellied stove. An educational unit was eventually added.

In 1912, a new church was built under the leadership of Pastor J.J. Parten. Construction was done by mostly donated labor. It would seat 250 people. A new education building was completed in 1947.

In 1955, lightning struck the building and it burned to the ground. The congregation, though facing hard economic times, was still able to construct a new building.

The church was fortunate to have had pastors that became strong denominational leaders such as Dr. Clifford Ingle, seminary professor; and missionaries Jeff Rousseau and Carl Rees.

Freedom Baptist Church, 1984

Freedom Baptist Church, 2017

Current Information

2201 North Summit Avenue
(417) 856-4271
www.Facebook.com/Freedom BaptistChurch

Resources Used

Bartee, Wayne C., *Greene County Baptist Churches in Ministry*, 1838-1984

Moser, Arthur Paul, *Churches of Greene County, MO*, 1983

The Churches of Springfield, Missouri, Springfield Area Council of Churches and the Springfield Ministerial Alliance, 1985

www.Facebook.com/Freedom BaptistChurch/

Immaculate Conception Catholic Church, 1868

After the Civil War, a growing population included a number of Catholics within the city. However, they were without a local place for worship. The church was organized on January 22, 1868, with Father Francis W. Graham serving as minister. On August 15, 1868, 110 Catholics met in Phelps Hall at the current site of the Woodruff Building on the downtown square of Springfield where Father Graham said the first mass. A new pastor, Father Theodore Kussman, began serving that same year and for another seventeen years. During his ministry, the congregation grew in number and a search began for new property on which to build. In 1874, on property purchased at the corner of Campbell and Tampa Streets, a cornerstone for the new building was laid. It served the parish for nearly ninety years.

A series of short-term pastorates ministered to the parish. During this time Immaculate Conception established the St. Joseph's Catholic Church with strict parish boundaries. With the coming of Father John Lilly in 1893, the church experienced a significant time of growth and infuluence in the community. Church indebtedness was eliminated and the prosperity continued during Father Lilly's twenty-three year

Immaculate Conception Catholic Church at the corner of Campbell and Tampa streets

Immaculate Conception Catholic Church at the corner of Fremont and Cherokee streets

pastorate. Father Dennis O'Driscoll came to the church in 1923, and remained for an eighteen-year pastorate. He led the church and the parishioners through the difficult financial times of the Great Depression.

From October 12, 1941 through September 11, 1955, Immaculate Conception was blessed with the pastoral leadership of Father Michael Baumgarten. In this challenging period, the church experienced the sacrificial actions of its parishioners in World War II and the Korean Conflict. Father Michael became a well-known figure in Springfield with his charitable nature and actions. In addition to the international crises, local challenges also faced the church. In his last year of service in September 1955, the old church structure was torn down after years of repair and upkeep.

On July 2, 1956, the new diocese of Springfield-Cape Giradeau was established and Springfield was designated as the Holy See. The first bishop appointed was the Most Reverend Charles Helmsing. There was a strong desire to move the church location closer to the area of city growth. Father Joseph Brody was appointed pastor in April 1957, to oversee the construction of a new church building on the northeast corner of Cherokee and Fremont. During construction, the auditorium of the St. John's School of Nursing was used for mass and church meetings. The first mass in the new building was held August 3, 1958. Under Father Brody's leadership, a school and convent were added as

Immaculate Conception Catholic Church, ca. 1990s.

Immaculate Conception Catholic Church, 2017

well as several new innovative church service programs.

A series of bishops and pastors served throughout the late 1960s and the 1970s. A 15-acre site was purchased on the northwest corner of Fremont Avenue and Primrose Street. The church property at Cherorkee Street and Fremont Avenue was sold to the St. John's Regional Health Center in May 1978. The next year, groundbreaking was held at the current site at 3555 South Fremont Avenue. Dedication was held on August 31, 1981; including education facilities, a gym, cafeteria and a priest's residence. The church had grown to a membership of over 1,150 by 1991. Two years later, the church added a new library, media center and a fine arts center. The parish community room was doubled in size and the church membership had grown to over 1,300 families.

In the early years of the 2000s, many building and office renovations were completed and the church was very active in meeting community needs. New methods of inner church membership communication were created allowing for better news and information. In the summer of 2009, major renovations were made in the office and reception rooms. New school facilities were completed in 2011.

The church of 1,100 continues its active participation in community ministry and educational programs.

Current Information

3555 South Fremont Avenue
(417) 887-0600
www.ic-parish.org/History.php

Resources Used

Fairbanks and Tuck, *Past and Present of Greene County, Missouri*, 1915

Pastva, Loretta, *The Catholic Church in Southern Missouri, 1956-2006*

Written history compiled by Dianne Hendley

www.ic-parish.org/History.php

Chapter Three

1870s

Historical Notes

The population of Springfield had grown to 7,000 and the city limits expanded south to Grand Street. The much anticipated arrival of the St. Louis-San Fransisco railroad came in 1870, extending from Rolla, Missouri. It came a mile and a half north of the square leading to the establishment of a new town, North Springfield, along Commercial Street. The dividing line between North and South Springfield was a road named Division Street. A decade later, the railroad was extended southward to the Old Town. Gas streetlights were added to the Square in 1875.

In 1871, the Sisters of Mercy, headquartered in Missouri at St. Louis, began expanding their work to other areas of Missouri. A 25-bed infrmary was opened in Springfield

In 1873, through the leadership of the local Congregational churches, Drury University was founded. They attempted to follow the lead of their other established universities, Dartmouth and Yale. Classes began in a single building on fewer than 1.5 acres.

In 1873, a national financial crisis and depression set back much of the city's growth and expansion. In 1874, the first train robbery in Missouri took place by the notorious James Gang. Their lawlessness and infamous reputation continued and gained national attention for the next eight years.

Comparatively fewer churches were established in this decade because of social unrest, financial instability, and maintaining existing church facilities. The need and support for black churches increased in the city as was evidenced by the church starts, although only a few were able to continue on their own.

Churches Established No Longer Qualifying

Dever Benton Avenue Methodist Episcopal Church, 1873
Benton Avenue A.M.E. Church, 1874

Sadly, one of the oldest churches ministering to blacks in the community had to close its doors in 2014. This long-established church had a distinguished history in the Springfield community. A frame building was erected in 1876, on the southeast corner of Benton Avenue and Center Street, directly opposite Stone Chapel of Drury College. An addition and new parsonage were built east of the sanctuary. The church endured the policies of segregation and social discrimination, common in the day. As other black churches in the city prospered, Benton Avenue began a decline in membership. In 2001, the church was placed on the National Register of Historic Places.

In 2014, the membership officially totaled three retired persons. Unable to continue its services and ministries, it had to close its doors July 1, 2014.

Zion Primitive Baptist Church, 1876

The group originally met in a hall near the public square. They later moved to a building on the southwest corner of Division and Inwood Streets.

Churches Currently Operating

No qualifying churches were found to be established in this decade.

Chapter Four

1880s

Historical Notes

Immaculate Conception Catholic Church, 2017

The 1880s witnessed the growth of new philosophies of government on an international level. Socialism and communism began their appeal in a time of economic depression and great cultural divide between the poor and the wealthy. In the United States, there was a great influx of immigrants from around the world. They brought with them their religious beliefs and cultural diversity. There was also a significant boom in what is called the American religions: Latter Day Saints, Jehovah's Witnesses, Seventh Day Adventists, Christian Scientists and other sectarian groups. Many of the mainline religious denominations experienced great expansion with new church starts.

Much of the nation was still in recovery from the Civil War. The telephone was invented in 1876, but it would be several decades before the new invention would be common to households and businesses. Springfield was impacted by these events as well as major economic developments. A decade earlier, the Pacific Railroad Company had been authorized by Congress to build a railroad line from Springfield, Missouri to the Pacific Ocean. Streetcar tracks were laid from the town square in all four directions. These streetcars were originally horse or mule drawn .

Much speculation was made by the purchase of land in both south and North Springfield. Eventually, it was decided that the railway would be located in North Springfield. The newly-established community of North Springfield began an intense rivalry with the city of Springfield.

It would be a number of years later, after several failed votes of unification, before the two communities would join together in 1887.

Churches Established No Longer Qualifying

First Swedish Baptist Church, 1882

They met in a frame structure at the corner of Campbell Avenue and Webster Street.

Central Congregational Church, 1883

German Congregational Church, 1884

They met originally in the Stone Chapel of Drury College with services conducted in German. In 1888, with financial help from a number of churches, the group built a new church building on Robberson Avenue, between Chestnut and Pine Streets.

First Methodist Church, 1885

Second Presbyterian Church, 1885

Mount Eagle Colored Baptist Church, 1886

Their building was located on Minor Street, a little to the east of Dollison. A brick building was erected in 1906.

Daily Memorial Methodist Episcopal Church, 1889

They met in a brick building on the northeast corner of Evans and Mount Vernon Streets.

Churches Currently Operating

Sacred Heart Catholic Church, 1882
Westminster Presbyterian Church, 1885
North Springfield Baptist Church, 1885
  Robberson Avenue Baptist Church, 1919
  Second Baptist Church, 1945
Salvation Army, 1885
St. John's (Protestant) Episcopal Church, 1886
Campbell (Street) United Methodist Church, 1886
South Street Christian Church, 1886
Macedonia Baptist Church, 1886
St. John's (German) Evangelical Church, 1887
  St. John's United Church of Christ, 1957
East Avenue Baptist Church, 1889
  National Heights Baptist Church, 1979
Boulevard Methodist Church, 1889
Mount Carmel United Methodist Church, 1920

Scared Heart Catholic Church, 1882

Sacred Heart Catholic Church

After several years of requests, a second Catholic church in North Springfield, Missouri, was sanctioned on May 27, 1882. There appears to have been some very visible opposition toward a second Catholic church in the city by some members of the Immaculate Conception Church. A peaceful cooperation was achieved through the cautious intervention of Father Kussman. Reverend Father Francis O'Neill was the first appointed pastor of the new parish. Without a church building, the small group of Catholic members met in residences and eventually on the ground floor of the new parish. The new sanctuary was originally named the St. Mary's Catholic Church and was completed for the first mass held on November 4, 1883.

A natural tragedy occurred on Monday, November 5, 1883. At 2:00 p.m. a strong tornado hit Springfield and "shattered the west wall of St. Mary's church, partially burying the tabernacle, demolishing upper portions of the south walls, uplifting and hurling the church roof to Locust Street, and leaving an appalling wake of wreckage, destruction and death..."

Reverend Father O'Neill appealed to other cities and the charity of local citizens to secure funds for the rebuilding of the church structure. It was rebuilt, renamed and dedicated as the Sacred Heart of Jesus. The first mass was held on June 8, 1884.

With a new pastor, Father B.F. Curran, the Sacred Heart School was established on June 18, 1887. In spite of his poor health, a number of new church organizations were begun to educate the membership and minister to the local community. A series of pastoral assistants aided the ailing pastor for the next fifteen years. In the 1910s, Father Daniel Healey became pastor. He may have been very instrumental in the Frisco Railroad locating their hospital in the parish near the church.

A longer-tenured pastor, Father Thomas J. Brady, arrived in April of 1920. He recounted later, "When I came here in 1920, there was $2.70 in the treasury, the church roof leaked and the basement of the church was full of water." He and the staff of four sisters lived with others in the distant Order of St. Agnes. A strike of local workers resulted in the loss of families in the community. Being "very cautious with money," Father Brady was able to purchase nearby housing, reroofed the building, had facility exteriors stuccoed, placed hardwood floors in the church and rectory, placed steam heating in the church and built a new school building. Father Brady remained at Sacred Heart for thirty-six years, retired in June 1956, and received the honor of being named the Very Reverend Monsignor.

In May 1957, major changes affected the Sacred Heart School. The population shifts had created a shortage of potential students and the students were transferred to the St. Joseph's School. Seminarians preparing for the priesthood lived in nearby housing and attended classes at the Regional Catholic High School. Another series of short-term pastors served the church during the late 1950s and early 1960s.

The 1970s found the Catholic churches adjusting to changes made by Pope John XXIII and the Second Vatican Council of 1965. The eleventh pastor of Sacred Heart, Father John W. Baker, had a challenging experience his first year with another facility crisis. He was informed

Sacred Heart Catholic Church

Sacred Heart Catholic Church, 2017

on the Saturday before the first Sunday of Advent that the ceiling of the church had just fallen. After quickly renting a nearby facility for the Sunday services and future meetings, Father Baker led the parish council to contract repairs on the structure.

In May 1974, Father Thomas Reidy, came to Scared Heart as pastor. He received notice that the House of Studies for seminarians was to be permanently closed in October of that year. Father Reidy conscientiously evaluated use of all the church facilities. He remodeled the House of Studies for church fellowships, made the other facilities more energy efficient, modernized the church heating system and improved the church grounds. On August 18, 1976, the Historical Site Board of Springfield voted to include the church on the Historical Register. A centennial celebration was held in 1982.

Contact Information

1609 North Summit Avenue
(417) 869-3646
www.sacredheart.org

Resources Used

Fairbanks and Tuck, *Past and Present Greene County, Missouri*, 1915

Pastva, Loretta, *The Catholic Church in Southern Missouri, 1956-2006*

www.associations.missouristate.edu/trails/historic_churches_in_springfield Sacred Heart Parish Centennial Book, 1882-1982, "*100 Years of Faith*", June 1982

www.sacredheart.org

Westminster Presbyterian Church, 1885-1915
Tabernacle Presbyterian Church, 1915-1936
Westminster Presbyterian Church, 1936

The early residents of Springfield were mostly devout Christians of many different beliefs. The Presbyterians found themselves with two churches in the city, First Cumberland Presbyterian organized in 1844, (the name changed to First Presbyterian in early 1900); and Calvary Presbyterian organized in 1849. Both originated from a Presbyterian Church in Cave Spring, Missouri, which is north of Willard. At the time of the Civil War, many churches found their congregations' loyalties divided between the North and South; and frequently they separated, forming new churches representing each side of the conflict. During the years of the Civil War, both of the Presbyterian churches in Springfield were loyal to the North.

In 1885, now twenty years after the conflict, a group of 41 members of the Calvary Presbyterian Church came forward as Southern sympathizers whose emotions were still running strong. They wanted to form their own Southern church. At their request, they were commended to a new organization affiliated with the Presbyterian Church in the United States and their obligations to Calvary ceased. This was the beginning of Westminster Presbyterian Church. The forming of the church was carried out in a dignified and agreeable manner with the new church being offered the use of the Calvary Church building for their meetings.

The formal organization of the church occurred on August 2, 1885. Their meetings were held in the courthouse on the public square of the city. The yet unnamed church began using the Westminster name in February 1886, and considered the need for a building. They found a lot at Elm and Jefferson Streets to their liking and it was purchased for the sum of $3,500.00. By year's end, the building was complete and they continued to use this building until 1913.

A small home adjacent to the church was purchased for use as a manse. (Manse is a home for the clergy in the Presbyterian Church.)

The city of Springfield had its own north-south battle at one time. The northern half of the city had encouraged officials of the Pacific

Westminster Presbyterian Church at the northeast corner of Elm and Jefferson

Railroad Company to lay tracks through their half of the city, which provided great advantage for attracting new businesses with a depot ready to receive freight and passengers. The south suffered as they lacked this advantage and there was no incentive to entice new businesses. The dividing line for the conflict was Division Street, and the feud and animosity between the two halves played out for years. The opening of railroad lines from Kansas City to Springfield in 1881, ended the feud and consolidated the city. The population of Springfield in 1897, stood at 23,267 people.

Two years prior to the organization of the Westminster Church, the nation was in the grip of an economic depression. As the years passed, the new church would suffer from its effects, but for now, they began to grow. The Session, the governing body of the Presbyterian Church, in their notes of 1895, state that 81 students attended Sunday School and weekly prayer meetings were well attended. However, two years later, in 1897, attendance began to drop.

The Westminster Church was now feeling the Depression. Hard financial times made meeting a pastor's salary a problem. A succession of pastors came and went. Some stayed less than a year, but not all left due to the economy. Some left for health reasons, stating they could not abide the climate in Springfield. The budget for the church was just $1,800, with $957.50 budgeted for the pastor and $5.00 designated for charity. By 1890, the Session made the decision to discontinue the Sunday night meetings because offerings were so small they could not cover the cost of keeping the lights on.

Financial conditions continued to decline. By September 1898, the church could only raise half of the salary due to the pastor and he was now considering another calling. This pastor, H.B. Boude, had served the struggling church for five years and his death, shortly thereafter, was an additional sorrow for the congregation. However, a new pastor was found and the church struggled on.

Finally, a discouraged Session petitioned the Presbytery to appoint and send to Springfield a commission to take such action as would be in the best interest of the church. The suggestion (possibly coming from the Presbytery) was that the church should once more consolidate with the Calvary Church. Those in the church refused this suggestion. They hoped the economy would improve enough for the church to continue and survive on its own, so they struggled on.

The mission spirit in the church was strong, and in 1906, a piece of property on Madison Street was purchased with the hope of building a chapel. The chapel would accommodate the state's newly acquired Normal School on Pickwick Street, adjacent to the property on Madison. (At the time privately-owned Springfield Normal School became a state institution known as State Normal School. Thereafter, it became State Teachers College and then Southwest Missouri State University). Due to continuing financial problems, the chapel was not built and, in 1908, then pastor, J.W. Jurey, instructed the property be sold and the money used to pay an outstanding bill for street paving.

By 1912, Springfield's economy did begin to improve but it was too late for the church. An effort was made to sell all the church property and purchase land for a church on the southwest corner of Cherry Street and National Avenue. The property was bought, but the dream to build a new church was never realized. Shortly after the completion of the purchase of the property, the church ceased all formal activity and became inactive, with the exception of the Session which, met even without an active congregation. The Women's Missionary Society continued to meet each month for fellowship, evangelizing, to study theology, and to help the needy.

In July of 1914, interest on the loan for the property on Cherry Street was due and the church was being pressed for the money. A Mrs. S.H. Charles offered to advance the money for the current amount owed and to look after future interest due on the note if the church would secure her. The Session voted to accept her offer without a dissenting vote. (No notes or details were given for how the Session secured Mrs. Charles.)

In January 1915, the church had been without a pastor for two years and there was only one ruling Elder. The Presbytery was urged to dispose of all the church's property, call for a pastor for the church, and begin to build a new church on the Cherry Street property as soon as possible.

So the end had come. Dedication, loyalty and determination had sustained the church through many hard times, but it was not enough. With no place to turn, in February of 1915 at a congregational meeting, a petition was brought forth to dissolve Westminster Church and organize a new Presbyterian Church. The Presbytery, under the direction of Reverend Trigg Thomas, dissolved all church property and a move to reorganize the church was begun. In May of 1915, a formal meeting was held to complete the dissolution of the church. One other disappointment faced the people of the church. The Westminster name was lost. During the two years of the church's inactivity, another church within the Presbytery had taken the Westminster name. Under reorganization, the church adopted the name Tabernacle Presbyterian.

Neither the Presbytery, nor the congregation of the now defunct Westminster Church, wanted to abandon the southern Presbyterian Church in Springfield. Now was the time for a fresh start, and to build a new church. In April of 1915, Reverend Grayson L. Tucker was called for the daunting task of reorganizing the church. Reverend Tucker rounded up the remnants of the old congregation and started recruiting new members. On April 16, 1915, the Tabernacle Presbyterian Church was formally organized. Reverend Tucker's outreach had worked and their numbers were growing. The original group of 149 included 21 baptized and 84 by transfer from other churches. The new church boasted Sunday School classes for children and adults.

The Tabernacle name was chosen for the tabernacle style building they constructed. The wooden structure was covered with tarpaper on the outside while two coal-burning stoves, one at each end, were used for heat. The pulpit stood on a raised platform at one end of the building.

In 1919, the congregation was ready for a larger building and it would be built on the Cherry Street property. Plans for the building were finalized the following year, and a new, red brick building was soon under construction. The church was still struggling financially, so bricks were added as the church could meet the expense. The building was of modest construction and the lower level was used before the auditorium level was completed. The final service in the Tabernacle building was held on August 21, 1921. The next month, a joyful congregation celebrated when stained glass windows to grace their new building were placed on order.

Reverend John Crockett, who served the church for 16 years, was a favorite with the youth of the church, the surrounding area and small towns. He successfully held many meetings to recruit new members and brought many people to the church. He was often called to preach in the small towns in the backwoods of the Ozarks. The Boy Scout Troop 16 at Tabernacle flourished under his direction and became one of the largest in town, attracting boys from other denominations. He left Tabernacle to accept the position of field representative for the School of the Ozarks.

The church was meeting its plans for growth under positive, dedicated leadership and the enthusiasm of the congregation. The new church building was dedicated in May 1928. However, they weren't done yet. They had plans for the growth and expansion of Tabernacle, but the Great Depression of 1929 forced them to postpone their plans. This time, the church was not alone in its economic struggle; the entire nation suffered with them.

Music was important to the church, and they raised their voices in the beautiful sounds of acapella singing or the music of a piano or treadle organ. In June of 1929, the Session considered a pipe organ, but it took another year before the organ was purchased for the cost of $2,000.00. The instrument came from a movie theater, as silent movies were becoming outdated and organ music was no longer used. The organ was of poor quality and not suited for the purpose intended. It was installed shortly before Dr. F.W. Bosch accepted a call to Tabernacle in February 1931. The organ, at Dr. Bosch's insistence, was removed because he said it was unsuited for the church's use and suffered "seriously from pneumonia." Music was an integral part of the worship service, so the organ was replaced with one more suited at a cost of $3,000.00, with money from a bank loan made in February 1932. Now, the church enjoyed soft, quiet, worshipful music. This organ was used in the church until 1985.

Dr. Bosch, who was considered a reserved man with a professional manner when he was installed, took a firm hand. He saw many improvements that he wanted to make. He was not happy with the choir because they wore too many colors and styles. He described them as looking like a flower garden and proposed they should have robes. The women of the church remedied this by getting together and making black robes with white linen collars that helped create a worshipful attitude.

In 1932, Dr. Bosch made a most unusual suggestion. He asked that the church reduce his salary the next year. His reasoning was twofold; they needed to pay for the new organ, and he wanted the Session to investigate the possibility of buying a manse on the installment plan.

As the years passed, much was accomplished in the church. Enhancing some programs and adding new ones, Dr. Bosch and his wife were enthusiastic in strengthening every aspect of Tabernacle Presbyterian Church.

The Presbytery announced to Tabernacle Church that their original name had once more become available and was free from conflict. So in June of 1936, the name was again changed to Westminster.

By 1939, the average Sunday School attendance was 315 people from a membership of 347. In addition that year, the annual report proudly stated that all bills were paid for the year. An advisory board was established to act as a clearinghouse for all problems within the church, but the Session remained the governing body.

Twenty-seven young men from the church entered the service in 1941, when the United States entered World War II. During the war years, membership in the church declined significantly, but the members gave freely of their time to help the war effort; working with the Red Cross, rolling bandages, and working at the USO. A red-letter day event was celebrated during this time with prayers of thanksgiving on December 20, 1942, when the mortgage papers on the building and the loan papers on the organ were burned.

One of Dr. Bosch's dreams was to sponsor a mission church, but in 1947, the Session decided that the youth of the church needed attention and built a "recreational hut" for youth activities. In 1953, the Session agreed to purchase property on Holland near Seminole at a cost of $12,500. There was no need at that time for a new church building as the current building on Cherry Street served their needs, but they were looking to the future when the church would need to expand, since the area where the church now stood had begun to become too commercial.

Westminster Church is proud of their principle of not holding bazaars, rummage sales or entertainments to raise money for the church's needs. The church almost never had financial difficulties. "We just say what we need and we seem to get it," said Dr. Bosch.

In 1955, the Session was ready to fulfill Dr. Bosch's dream for a new mission church and would use the Holland Street property. But before this was realized, Dr. Bosch became ill, and his consequent death devastated the congregation. After a month of grieving for their pastor, it was time to move ahead with their plans and the search for a new pastor would begin.

Westminster Presbyterian Church at Portland Street

Dr. Bosch served the church for 25 years. During his career, he contributed not only to Westminster Presbyterian, but also throughout the Springfield community. He brought an intense belief in education as a part of religion. He taught the Bible as it should apply to everyday life.

In March of 1955, a building committee made up of members of Westminster, Calvary, and First Presbyterian was formed, as the other churches had agreed to join in the building of a new church on the South Holland lot. In December, Westminster notified Calvary and First Presbyterian that only their congregation would build the new church. The mission church was ready for its congregation around January of 1957, and plans to complete the transfer of the title and members to the new church on South Holland were formulated. Forty adult members and their families from Westminster formed the nucleus of the congregation. Westminister had considered moving its entire congregation to the new church rather than form the mission church but this idea was voted down. Thus, the mission church was on its own, with the help of the Presbytery, who sent a pastor to work on the organization and development.

In July of 1955, a new pastor was installed at Westminster Presbyterian, Reverend H. Leland Murphy. The Session purchased property at 1057 E. Stanford to serve as a manse. In October of 1958, due to ill health, Reverend Murphy left the church and another search for a pastor was begun. Reverend Charles Brown was chosen and installed in September of 1959. Reverend Brown's youthful vigor attracted young people and families to the church. Membership, which had begun to decrease through the time when pastors and interim pastors were at the church, was once more growing.

The church building at National Avenue and Cherry Street was beginning to show its age and needed upgrading and repairs. The space within the building had become inadequate as the congregation grew, and it was becoming more and more difficult to continue in the existing space. The widening of the street at the corner of the building brought traffic noise and the stench of exhaust fumes within a few feet of the front door, which began to disrupt services. Parking was now at a premium, as the widening of the street reduced the parking space. Street parking was relied on more and more. Early in 1961, an expansion committee reported that plans to acquire adjoining property for expansion and to complete needed repairs would cost $185,000, but that would not resolve all of their existing problems. It was reported that property was available at Portland and Delaware Streets for the sum of $45,000 and a building could be constructed at a cost of $109,000. On March 12, 1961, the congregation gave overwhelming approval with 131 "go votes", which gave the Session permission to proceed.

The financial status of the church didn't support this project, as there was only a fraction of the $45,000 needed to purchase the lot, and nothing to support the building of the church. Drops in membership, though beginning to rise again, had hurt finances of the church and the condition of the church building itself was a detriment to its growth.

There was opposition to the building plan, but a sturdy band of members supported the plan with optimism and Christian hope. A building council was formed, headed by strong and vocal members of the congregation who, through their actions and belief in the plan, brought everyone together behind the project.

For a time, the style of the new building was in contention. Some wanted a timeless building of cut stone or a red-brick-white-steeple style edifice. However, the building needed an economic design to meet the 20th Century. The traditionalists yielded and their concerns for the design of the church proved unnecessary. The lot at Delaware and Portland was approved for purchase by the Session in September of 1961.

Raising the money for the building would take a great deal of sacrifice on the part of the congregation, and years to save the money. They needed a simple answer for a plan to accomplish the goal. "The new building," they said, "will cost approximately 25 cents a square foot. Even the young members can make an important contribution to a new church. It all starts here...189,000 square feet at 25 cents per square foot. How many square feet can you purchase?" The congregation got behind this idea and certificates suitable for framing were given to each member who contributed, naming the amount of square footage for which they paid .

An architect was hired in March of 1962, but when time came to purchase the lot, they were $15,000 short of the cost of $45,000. At that time, Skelly Oil Company bought the lot at National and Cherry and gave the church 18 months to vacate. Now all the "Doubting Thomases," who saw the idea of building a new church as a financial risk, breathed a sigh of relief that the money for the project would be available.

The plans and design presented by the architect were approved, but not before much discussion on the decision of where to put the choir. Agreement was finally reached, with the choir in the chancel, and the building design chosen would be of contemporary design, based on the desires of the congregation.

Of course, like most projects of this size, the final cost would run over the budget, and in February 1963, the congregation was greeted with this information. It was decided that the additional funds needed would be borrowed. A builder was hired, and following Easter Sunday worship service, 200 people gathered at the Portland Street property for the groundbreaking of the new building.

With the cornerstone laid, the building was ready to be occupied. On December 22, 1963, the first worship service was held. Now there was space to accommodate all that the church wanted, with room for expansion. Plenty of parking spaces were available in the lot, so no street parking would be necessary.

Membership continued to grow under Reverend Brown. By the end of 1964, it had reached 508, with Church School attendance for adults and children averaging 354 each Sunday. Due to the success of the Church School, space was at a premium to accommodate all the classes. Once again, a Building Committee was elected to investigate the addition of an educational wing. With the approval granted, the added space placed an additional 45 feet on the north wing of the church, which was dedicated in December of 1965.

The success of the church was undisputed as new and varied activities were started. Many of these activities were designed to put the congregation members, adults and children alike, in the community to assist and help with many worthy causes. The social aspects of the congregation were addressed with multiple occasions for the adults to enjoy the fellowship of others within the congregation. A Men's Breakfast and Bible Study was also established and was well attended. All of these activities became too much for Reverend Brown to manage alone, and in March of 1969, an associate pastor, Reverend Jim Ainsworth, was installed.

After a ministry of 10 years at the church and the membership standing at 646, Reverend Brown presented his resignation. Though the resignation was a disappointment for the church and the Brown family would be missed, the church was fortunate to have Reverend Ainsworth for the next five years.

A bequest to the church of $70,000 was used to add a youth building onto the church. By July 1970, it was completed, and opened on Saturday nights for the youth of the community and the church. Music, which was sometimes quite loud, and food were offered. The project became known as "Granny's." One night, as many as 476 youth attended the popular event, which necessitated limiting attendance to 400. The fifty-cent admission fee was ample to cover expenses and support other programs. Though successful, and attended by adults, and by three police officers to keep order, a decision to discontinue the program became necessary, as the responsibilities were too great for the church to shoulder alone.

Boy Scout Troop 16 started at the church in 1919, and continued to become the oldest troop in the city with 860 members. The Girl Scout Troop 71 has been associated with Westminster since 1970. Both groups make good use of the added Youth Building in the church.

Reverend Jim Ainsworth's service was well accepted at the church and he is credited with many improvements. However, according to Presbyterian law, an associate pastor cannot become the pastor in the same church they are serving. With sadness, the congregation wished Reverend Ainsworth and his family well as they made their way to a new home in Texas. With his resignation submitted in October of 1974, and after a search of six months, Reverend Jim Forkner and his family were welcomed to Westminster in May of 1975.

Reverend Jim Forkner submitted his resignation in 1983 and thereafter several interim pastors served the church. The most notable, who served for a year, was Dr. Silas Kessler. Dr. Kessler, though retired in 1976, felt he still had the energy and the will to serve. He and his wife traveled and served in different churches throughout the country, with their stays lasting one year. In 1963, Dr. Kessler served as the Moderator of the General Assembly of the Presbyterian Church (USA), which is the highest elective office in the denomination. At the end of Dr. Kessler's year, which is all that is allowed in the church for an interim pastor, it was decided to accept the call of another interim pastor instead of a permanent pastor.

The next pastor, Reverend James Robinson, was no stranger to the congregation as he had preached at the church many times. He served and contributed to the National Presbyterian conference, in 1983, as a delegate. This conference was responsible for uniting the northern and southern branches of the church for the first time since the Civil War. On Friday, June 10, 1983, The Presbyterian Church (USA) was formally constituted at 8:37 p.m. in a service of Holy Communion. Fourteen thousand people shared in the service. The church now existed with 3,166,062 members and 13,225 churches.

During Dr. Robinson's time at the church, the centennial year was celebrated with daylong festivities. A picnic on the church grounds was planned where some members attended in the costumes of the 1880s. Other activities and games for the children reminiscent of the era when the church was first organized, were followed by an old fashioned hymn singing in the church.

Westminster is proud of the library they have assembled over the years and it was given a space of its own after the church moved to its present location. Tables and shelving were donated to the church and the Boy Scout Troop took on the project of cataloging the books that had been donated or purchased over the years. Christian education is emphasized in the church, and the library has a large selection of books on Bible reference.

The subject of acquiring an organ, (actually the two organs that were discussed earlier) now led to the acquisition of yet another organ. When the organ was moved to the new location at Portland and Delaware, it suffered major damage and any repairs made proved to be expensive as well as faulty, so the organ needed to be replaced. A fundraising effort was begun with success far exceeding expectations and the new instrument was purchased. Music is an important part of life at Westminster and they celebrated the new organ's arrival, after a complicated installation, with a concert on April 14, 1985, performed by Dr. Delbert Disselhorst, a concert organist.

For some time now, the church had been served and led by an interim pastor. Around this time, January 1985, a permanent pastor would be sought. Abiding by the standards of excellence set by the Presbytery, the search for a new pastor became more complicated than in years past. The nomination committee prepared a Mission Study Report, which outlined the goals and concerns of the church and made an up-to-date study report of the church. Many different groups within the church contributed information. After an exhaustive amount of time, work, and effort by the committee, Dr. Ron Stewart was asked to pastor the church. He had a strong Presbyterian background that placed a high value on Christian education. When his name was offered to the congregation, they responded with an almost unanimous vote.

Dr. Stewart had grown up close to where the church stood and so he was familiar with the neighborhood. The reorganization of committees of the deacons and the Session was just one of his accomplishments, as was the installation of air conditioning for the church and the offices. Many programs were started and improvements completed during Dr. Stewart's time at the church. Midway through his tenure, his wife was diagnosed with cancer, and managing the responsibilities of his family, his wife, and his duties in the church became complex. After serving for 17 years, he made the difficult decision to resign.

Now two search committees began their work, one seeking an interim pastor and one looking for the right person as a permanent pastor. During this time, the worship committee performed the weekly service. The search committee, looking for an interim pastor, found Reverend John Nipper as an excellent choice, and he began his ministry on September 15, 2001. Periods of confusion and questioning always occur when a new leader is installed, but Reverend Nipper seemed the perfect person to guide the congregation through this time of change. He was a prayerful man, who encouraged the congregation to pray for the committee as they looked for a new pastor. Not coming to the church to make changes, he drew the congregation together to hold onto the important things the church had: Sunday worship, music, Sunday School, and Vacation Bible School. He asked the congregation to respect and support each other, take care of the facility, and continue with hope and faith.

The search committee spent many hours looking for the new pastor with hundreds of phone calls made, many resumes read, meetings held, and candidates interviewed. When the committee met Ellen Brantley and heard her preach, they felt that their search for a permanent pastor was ending, and they began to relax.

Ellen Brantley was welcomed into the church on August 15, 2003. She and her family were an exciting addition to the Westminster congregation. Pastor Ellen hit the ground running, and immediately understood that this "new" church building was, in fact, now 40 years old and in need of upkeep. A priority list was made, and the chores and changes began. From refurbishing buildings, to adding ceiling fans and light fixtures, and updating the narthex by adding the stained glass windows salvaged from the Cherry Street church, nothing was overlooked. Once again, one of the most important tasks was attention to the organ, which received a complete restoration.

The building's physical changes that Pastor Ellen initiated were necessary, but the worship and mission aspects of the church that she started have been much appreciated. A Parents' Day Out program was started to help relieve the stressed-out mothers and fathers of the church. A plan was drawn up and approved by the State of Missouri for the program, which has brought new congregants to the church. A program for young adults with children to offer them fellowship in the church has created a lively church school and children's choir. They are a great hope for the future of Westminster Presbyterian Church.

Pastor Ellen fostered a relationship with nearby Delaware School, serving lunch to the teachers and offering assistance with whatever

Westminster Presbyterian Church, 2017

may be needed at the school. This allowed the congregation the opportunity to work in the community. When asked what role the church should take, Pastor Ellen stated that education is the most important and this is what the church should accomplish.

Westminister is active in both John Calvin Presbytery and the Synod of Mid-America. Many of its members have served on its committees, as has the pastor. The Presbyterian Church is a connectional church. The church supports Well of Life in the city. This group supports families in need, particularly in the center of the city.

Now the church, a decade into the new century, is watching the world change. There is faith that the Lord will lead them into a future of greener and greener pastures. The story of this church is one of triumph, persistence, and accomplishment. Throughout their history, their love of God, their welcoming spirit, and their sense of family and faith can be seen. All is centered on Christ. Westminster has met all challenges, both the positive and negative, with determination, devotion, leadership, and a committed congregation. The march into the future will be the same.

Current Information

1551 East Portland Street
(417) 866-2711
www.westminsterspmo.com

Resources Used

Fairbanks and Tuck, *Past and Present Greene County*, 1915

Westminster Presbyterian Church, 1885-2010- A History (second edition)

www.westminsterspmo.com

North Springfield Baptist Church, 1885 Robberson Avenue Baptist Church, 1919 Second Baptist Church, 1945

Robberson Avenue Baptist Church

The history of most churches has many twists and turns affected by geographic location, economic developments, and leadership within and outside of the church. Such was the case of this church. It had three name changes, as many locations, and experienced many levels of economic development.

Many churches begin their history as mission efforts with financial support from the sponsoring church. That was not the case with this church. In 1882, a group of four influential men, who were members of the First Baptist Church, felt the need to begin a new church in the developing North Springfield area. They contacted Edwin T. Robberson, who had invested in much of the land in that area. The group requested land for the construction of a new church. Dr. Robberson donated land at the corner of Booneville Avenue and Webster Street. They also enlisted the pastor of First Baptist Church, W.A. Nelson, to preach on Sunday afternoons and Thursday evenings. The small group of worshippers met at several locations while a permanent building was being planned. They met at the Templar's Hall and the Grand Army of the Republic on Commercial Street. They enlisted a pastor from Minnesota, Reverend John H. Thompson, in 1884. The group rented the Frisco Opera House for regular services. On March 1, 1885, the church was officially organized as the North Springfield Baptist Church. During this time, the church did not receive any financial assistance from a sponsoring church. It was able to become financially self-sufficient.

Exterior of the second building, erected 1917

With church growth steadily on the rise, it became necessary for a new building. The previous site donated by Dr. Robberson was now deemed inadequate. A new site, several blocks from the Frisco Opera House, at 1616 North Robberson Avenue, was desired. Dr. Robberson graciously bought back his earlier donated land for the price of the land at the new desired location. On Sunday, July 4, 1886, the church's first building was completed and dedicated. Many now called the church the Robberson Avenue Baptist Church.

On April 4, 1887, unification of North Springfield with Springfield was approved in a supportive city vote: 2,519 for and 71 against. Now the church began an identity crisis, with a name reminding many of the past division. There was confusion locally and statewide regarding the official name of the church. Finally, on January 4, 1905, the church officially changed its public name to that commonly used, the Robberson Avenue Baptist Church. To add to the confusion, it was agreed to keep the legal name as North Springfield Baptist Church on all official documents. This continued to create confusion on the part of the local media and state denominational leaders. It was not until March 4, 1959, that the name issue was resolved. The church voted to adopt the public and legal name of the Second Baptist Church. This was actually the second "Second Baptist Church" in Springfield history. An earlier black church, started by First Baptist Church in 1867, was named the Second Baptist Church. After years of deeming the name "second" demeaning, that church changed its name, in 1904, to the Washington Avenue Baptist Church.

The early work of the North Springfield Baptist Church continued in its mission of outreach and expansion. Two missions were started and grew into strong churches on their own. The East Avenue Baptist

Second Baptist Church, 2017

Church (currently National Heights Baptist Church) was organized in 1889. The Ray Chapel Baptist Church (currently Hamlin Memorial Baptist Church) was organized in 1892.

Development of church buildings during the church's history was a result of good leadership and economic prosperity. By early 1917, the church had outgrown its first building. It was decided to tear down the building and go back to the Frisco Opera House while new construction was underway. The first services in the new building were held on June 23, 1918. Through the challenges of a national economic depression and two world wars, the building was becoming difficult to repair.

After considerable investigation of the community growth patterns, the church decided to build a new sanctuary, in a new location on a five acre plot at the corner of Oak Grove Avenue and Catalpa Street, on property that was owned by the Greene County Baptist Association. The groundbreaking was on May 8, 1960. The first service was held on Easter, April 2, 1961, with the dedication on July 2. A library and Sunday School rooms were added in 1964, and a gymnasium and second floor were added in January 1969. Additional staff was added in the following years to aid in a growing church ministry. Surrounding properties were purchased for future parking and building expansion.

The church's fourth new sanctuary was dedicated on December 14, 1980.

In 1990, the church moved to its present location on East Battlefield Street.

Current Information

3111 East Battlefield Street
(417) 887-3111
www.secondbaptist.org/about

Resources

(Much of the information was from summaries of materials graciously provided during a personal interview in 2015 with current Pastor John Marshall.)

75 Years of Spiritual Service, A History of Second Baptist Church, 1885-1961, Diamond Jubilee, by the History Committee: Mr. And Mrs. Bentley Keen and Mr. Cecil B. Keen

Bartee, Wayne C., *Greene County Churches in Ministry, 1838-1984*

Celebrating 100 Years, 1885-1985, Second Baptist Church, Springfield, Missouri, by Barbara Merrick Southwick

Fairbanks and Tuck, *Past and Present Greene County, Missouri,* 1915

Moser, Arthur Paul, Churches of Springfield, MO, *1983*

Second Baptist Church, Springfield, Missouri, 1885-1900, by Dr. John E. Marshall, for the Quasquicentennial edition, 1885-2010

www.secondbaptist.org/about/

Salvation Army, 1885

We had hoped to include more information about this organization. Yet, after repeated contact attempts, the organization has not responded to our requests for information on their organizational history. We have found some limited information from secondary sources that we have included.

The Salvation Army is unique in its identity as a religious group. It is not an official church and is not identified as a denomination. It is an international, religious organization that has a widespread recognition throughout the United States. Although the local Springfield operation was acknowledged to have begun in 1885, any recorded history of their local operations is unavailable. It will be important to note their international beginning, their movement to the United States, and, eventually, to Missouri.

The organization can trace its founding to William and Catherine Booth in London, England, in 1852. Disappointed with the local church's rejection of the poor, homeless, hungry, and destitute people of England, the couple began a ministry. After a successful tent revival in 1865, in the East End of London, the organization attracted followers and the attention of some local churches. Their primary aim was evangelism and ministering to human needs. The end goal was to unite these people with a local church for ministry and nuturing. By 1867, they had ten full-time workers. By 1874, the Booths had 1,000 volunteers and 42 evangelists serving under the banner of "The Christian Mission." The followers referred to William Booth as "General" and the organization became known as the "Hallelujah Army." Booth penned the name "Salvation Army" in 1878.

Salvation Army, 2017

The movement, now growing worldwide, came to the United States in the person of Lieutenant Eliza Shirley. She left England to join her parents, who had immigrated earlier. In 1879, she held the first meeting of the Salvation Army in Philadelphia and was received very well by the community. On March 10, 1880, an official delegation of eight workers arrived in New York at Battery Park. Their work did not receive a good welcome, and a series of personal attacks followed. In spite of that, they expanded their work into twelve states, including Missouri, with much more success. After an unsuccessful beginning in St. Louis, Missouri, the organization found greater acceptance in Springfield, in 1885. William Oliver was the first head of the Springfield Salvation Army, serving for several years until he was appointed relief officer of the city. The organization "provided food and clothing for the needy, and in other ways seeking to minister to the sorrows and sins and needs, physical and spiritual, of their fellow men, especially the poor and those 'down and out' to whom the churches, even when desiring to do so, find it practically almost impossible to render helpful personal ministry."

By 1886, President Grover Cleveland received a delegation of Salvation Army officers and gave the organization his personal, strong endorsement.

Current Information

1707 West Chestnut Expressway
(417) 862-5509
www.facebook.com/SalvationArmyOzarkArea

Resources Used

www.salvationarmyusa.org/usn/history-of-the-salvation-army

St. John's (Protestant) Episcopal Church, 1886

The Reverend Octavious Parker was the Rector of the Christ Church, which was established in Springfield in 1859. He was concerned with the burden of the distance the residents of North Springfield traveled to attend services in his church on Walnut Street. He took the concern seriously and made the decision to bring the church to the people. With that goal in mind, he purchased property in 1881, at the corner of Boonville Avenue and Park Street. The Ozark Land Company asked the sum of $50.00 for the property and generously gave Rector Parker the adjoining lot free.

Occasional services were held for this new church and a Sunday school was established, but no records of where the services were held were found. Continuous activity was not recorded until the Reverend W.H. Osborne became the rector of Christ Church. He saw, as Reverend Parker had before him, that the congregants in North Springfield needed a parish of their own.

On March 29, 1886, after evening prayer meeting, Rector Osborne conducted the first meeting of St. John's Episcopal Church. This first meeting was held at the Good Templar's Hall on Commercial Street in Springfield. The Canonical Articles of Association were established, and a vestry was elected at this meeting. Twenty-two of those in attendance signed the Articles of Association.

The parish was admitted to the union of the Council of Diocese of Missouri at a gathering on May 26, 1886. The Reverend Melville M. Moore was asked to take the position of rector on May 31, 1886. Reverend Moore came from Holy Trinity Church in Nashville, Tennessee.

The rector-elect, Melville Moore, visited the parish and held services on the morning of Trinity Sunday, June 20, 1886. The service was held in the Wall Building on Commercial Street. The service included prayer, sermon and Holy Communion. A chancel platform was arranged and an altar of crude packing boxes was used. The boxes were covered with a white cloth and artfully arranged with flowers and vines. Thirty-two persons attended the service. A service was also held that evening, and well attended by seventy-six people, with Rector Moore

St. John's Episcopal Church with its first addition, 1892

again officiating. Great hope was placed on this beginning and the services were met with hearty enjoyment.

The Merriman Building on the corner of Commercial Street and Robberson Avenue was the location for the first regular service, which was on August 8, 1886. Rector Moore accepted the call to serve the new church at this meeting. The Merriman Building was prepared for the service with the presentations of a small altar, lectern, desk, and stall made by the Ladies Social Club of North Springfield, many of whom were parishioners.

The vestry of the Episcopal Church is the legal representative of the parish in all matters regarding corporate property. As such, a letter was sent by the vestry of St. John's Church to Christ Church requesting the lots purchased on Boonville Street be given to St. John's for a new parish. The request, however, was not favorably received and relinquishing of the lots was denied. This continued with several letters being passed between the two churches. After multiple exchanges, a decision regarding the lots had still not been reached. The chancellor of the Diocese of Missouri intervened and resolved the conflict by giving the lots to St. John's.

A building fund was started, and preparations were underway to construct a permanent home for St. John's. Now it was decided that the Boonville lots were in an area that was becoming too commercial. The lots were sold for $1,825.00 and the money was used to purchase two lots on the corner of Benton Avenue and Division Street. The deeds for the lots were filed on May 18, 1887 and the sum of $3,000.00 was paid.

Former vestrymen, Mr. B.F. Hobart, gave the building fund a boost by pledging to give $1,000.00 for every $3,000.00 raised by the congregation. To hasten the donations, he placed a deadline of July 1887 on his pledge. He also started the giving off with a donation of $1,200.00.

Sacred vessels were one of the first needs of the church. A request went out for donations of precious metals, including gold and silver, for the vessels. The request also included jewels to embellish the vessels. This was met with great success by the congregants and Rector Moore gave praise for the items donated. He also remarked that the beauty and richness of the Communion service would be cherished by those who had given so freely.

Now that the building fund was well underway, the plans for a building were needed. Mr. Kivas Tully was named as architect and a contract for the building was formalized. The foundation of the church was laid in November of 1887.

During this time, St. John's was asked to relinquish the use of the service room in the Merriman Building where the church had been meeting. Services were moved to a room at the Bank of Springfield at the corner of Commercial Street and North Jefferson Street. For some of the time prior to the completion of the church building, they also met in a storeroom on Commercial Street, which had at one time housed a butcher shop.

When the initial building fund ended in July of 1887, a total of $8,229.81 was raised and $8,231.45 was used for the building, land, and equipment. The new building was completed in 1888 and was built in the English-Gothic style. The furnishings are of polished oak in the gothic style and the altar is of polished oak. The church could support a capacity of 210 congregants. The chancel, the choir, and the sanctuary are separated by a polished walnut altar rail.

The windows are of colored mosaic cathedral glass with a rose window that is in the gothic style. The rose window takes the form of an open rose and has a central medallion with a central motif of the cross of Christ with the letters "JHF," (Jesus Hominum Falzatum), the earliest symbol of the Christian Church first found in the catacombs at Rome. This window is reputed to be the only true rose window west of the Atlantic seaboard. The first service of the new church was held on September 23, 1888.

The new church building was complete and the new rector had settled into life in Springfield, including his marriage to one of the church members. However, as time passed, it became apparent that the building was not meeting the needs of the church as its membership grew. Some of the organizations within the church were feeling the need for more space to allow for meetings and gatherings. One of these groups, The Brotherhood of St. Andrew, which focuses on prayer, Bible study, and service to the community, played an active role in the addition of the church. The Ollis brothers donated the $250.00 to add new walls to the church. This work was completed at a cost of $377.50 in May of 1892.

A financial panic that affected the entire nation in 1893 also caused financial difficulties for the church. The church was unable to meet its obligations and make payments. The holder of the mortgage was pressing for back amounts due and had threatened to have the property advertised for sale and forced into foreclosure. Rector Moore made a plea to the congregation and sent out 1,500 appeals around the country for assistance, as well as sending an appeal to 40 rectors of large parishes for their assistance. These appeals netted a total of $785.00. Rector Moore donated $25.00 to start the appeal to the parishioners, who ultimately responded with donations of $1,800.00. Once again the ladies of the church stepped up to help the cause by holding dinners, bazaars, bake sales, and other activities to help raise the funds needed. The children helped by giving generously of their dimes, nickels, and pennies. The appeals ultimately raised $2,300.00, and the mortgage was paid off. With the indebtedness against the church satisfied, the Consecration of St. John's Church was held on St. Mark's Day, Wednesday, April 25, 1894. In March of that year, the Parish Record showed 123 communicants in the eight years since the organization of the church. Many other occurrences were also noted such as marriages, deaths, baptisms, and confirmations.

In April of 1898, Rector Moore tendered his resignation from the church, as he and his wife were moving to California for his health. It was with great regret that the congregation accepted the resignation and the search for a new rector was started. During this time, when the church was without a rector, the Ollis brothers were instrumental in serving as lay readers until a new rector could be found. It was reported that Rector Moore died just two years after leaving the church.

The search for a new rector ended when Reverend Walter S. Trowbridge was hired in the fall of 1898. He was a single man, and rather than have him live in a hotel, a room was built for his use in the northeast corner of the Parish. He used the room for two years, paying rent of $10.00 per month, which is the amount a hotel would have charged him.

In March of 1984, the following notice could be found in "The Parish Helper", a parish newspaper, "We ask some of our boys to kindly remember that when they enter the Church, it should not be done in a noisy manner. Tread lightly, not as if the House of God were a public building or a sawmill. Parents will kindly read this item to their boys – from 6 to 20 years old."

A rectory was built on the southwest corner of the church property. Shortly after, Rector Trowbridge married and brought his new wife to the church from her home in Illinois. He tendered his resignation in December of 1904. The church went through a series of rectors who stayed for short terms, due to circumstances that were extraordinary. Reverend Robert Nelson Spencer was called from Salina, Kansas late in 1906. He stayed for three years, and was instrumental in building the membership of the church and organizing auxiliaries and guilds to serve the church. He eventually became Bishop of the Diocese of West Missouri. Several members of the congregation traveled to Kansas City for Reverend Spencer's consecration.

On April 30, 1906, the bishop of the diocese asked for a special offering to give relief for the victims of the San Francisco earthquake, where over 3,000 people had died and 80% of the city was destroyed.

Through the decade of 1910 to 1920, several rectors came to serve at the church. It was reported that in approximately 1915, the membership of the church reached 189 with 84 in the Sunday School. There were many organizations for missionary and parish work, with an aggregate of 82 members.

In August of 1923, a memorial service was held at St. John's Church. It was conducted at the same hour that funeral services were being conducted for the late President Warren G. Harding. The program was noteworthy in that a service of this nature had never been conducted in Springfield. There were no sounds of voices except in the songs and in one prayer delivered by Reverend William H. Talmadge. The remainder of the service was conducted in pantomime. Reverend Talmadge had come to the church in 1923, and resigned under pressure of the vestry after four years of service.

In October 1927, The Reverend Lewis R. Anschutz came to the church and served for the next 18 years. He was praised for his singing voice. As a boy in New York City, he was a member of the first boy's choir in the Cathedral of St. John the Divine. Reverend Anschutz had, at one time,

St. John's Episcopal Church in 1925

served at a parish in Hyde Park, New York. It was here that he became acquainted with the Franklin D. Roosevelt family. It was at the same time President Roosevelt was stricken with polio. A considerable intimacy developed between the two families, and Mrs. Roosevelt brought the Reverend and his family fresh produce from her garden.

In December of 1930, Reverend Anschutz made a yearbook and directory for the parish. He listed all the improvement and repairs that had been made to the church over the previous two years, at a cost of $3,800.00. A boys' choir was organized in December of 1930, and performed at a Christmas program at the church. During this same time, Reverend Anschutz was serving an Episcopal mission in Lebanon, Missouri. Easter service, in 1930, had the largest attendance on record in the history of the church, with 500 attending.

The golden anniversary of the church was held on March 22, 1936. Reverend Walter S. Trowbridge, second rector to serve the parish, was the celebrant at services and the guest of honor at a supper for members and former members. Reverend Anschutz reported to the parish, in October of 1936, that during his nine years with the church he had baptized 176 persons, presented 186 for confirmation, solemnized 97 marriages, and officiated at 198 burials.

Members of St. John's Church decided, in February of 1942, to forego construction of new quarters, and instead use the $850.00 accumulated to buy defense bonds. The Easter letter from Reverend Anschutz mentions that 37 young men from the parish were in service to the nation.

Sadness struck the church when Reverend Anschutz unexpectedly suffered a fatal heart attack at the rectory on September 8, 1945, at the age of 55. His death was a tremendous loss to the community. He is said to have taken great pride in the church building with its beautiful rose window, and often contributed by helping to clean and polish the church for festive celebrations.

The church was without a rector for three months until December 2, 1945. Canon Everett J. Downes was chosen by the bishop to become priest-in-charge of St. John's Parish. After coming to St. John's, he promoted activities in youth organizations and took part in civic affairs. He was highly recognized for his activities and interest for the youth by the parish, the diocese and the city of Springfield. He was with the parish until he resigned in May of 1948.

A parochial stewardship campaign in the Episcopal Church invited members to pledge to the church for the following year, not only their money, but also their time and their talents. For the year 1946, financial pledges were made of $6,238.00. These pledges represented only a small part of the membership of the church making it difficult to prepare a budget.

In 1947, the Presiding Bishop's Fund for World Relief began a drive for relief for war-torn Europe. The diocese's share was to be $5,000.00.

The church had a new rector in 1948, Harold Whitehead, after Canon Downes resigned.

In 1949, the church purchased a house on nearby Benton Avenue, at a cost of $17,500.00. The house, an eight-room structure, would be used for needed additional space. Also during this time, a campaign was launched to construct an educational wing to the church building. This was a longtime goal that had been put aside due to the Great Depression, and then, World War II. A two-story addition was planned for the church and a goal of $80,000.00 was needed in pledges. The construction was completed in 1958, when the cornerstone was laid. The addition contained classrooms, a kitchen, and an addition to the sacristy. The cost was $71,300.00, partially covered by the issuance of bonds. With the growth of the city to the southeast, an additional parish was needed for Springfield. Parishioners of St. John's and Christ Church aided in the establishment of the mission. The first service was held at St. James Mission on June 14, 1959.

Many changes and updates to the church were completed through the decades of the 1970s, which included renovations to the parish hall

St. John's Episcopal Church, 2017

and the repair of all the stained glass windows in the lower part of the church (then protected with plexiglass). The parish celebrated the 77th anniversary of the consecration of the church in April of 1971. In May of 1978, St. John's Episcopal Church was presented a plaque designating it as a historic site.

The Reverend Daren K. Williams accepted the call to become the 16th rector of St. John's in March of 1986, which was shortly before the centennial of the founding of the church celebration on May 25, 1986. Many members, former members, civic leaders of Springfield, and State Senator Dennis Smith, were present. The event included a special liturgy and luncheon.

A beautiful statue of the Blessed Virgin Mary was placed on the west lawn of the church property in 1991. The statue, from Italy, is created from Carrara marble. A memorial garden built at its base has been a focus for blessings at different times and for private prayers. In the future, the site will be used as a columbarium for the interment of ashes of members at their request.

In 2011, the 125th anniversary of St. John's was planned with a year-long celebration. A DVD production of the history of the church was created for the celebration. Events included a Founders' Day picnic, and the planting of an oak tree. The finale of the event was a Solemn Evensong followed by a dinner and the installation of a time capsule.

As St. John's moves into the future, it will continue to grow and be a shining example of faith, sacrifice, prayer, caring, and devotion in the city of Springfield.

Current Information

515 East Division Street
(417) 869-6351
www.stjohnsspringfield.diowestmo.org/history

Resources Used

Fairbanks, Jonathan and Tuck, Clyde Edwin, *Past and Present of Greene County Missouri*. Springfield Greene County Library

Historical Postcards of Springfield, Missouri – Springfield Greene County Library

St. John's Episcopal Church (Springfield, Missouri) –Wikipedia.org

Twelve Decades – *A History of St. John's Episcopal Church of Springfield, Missouri*, Prepared for the Centennial of Consecration of the Church by Maurice Bostwick

Campbell (Street) United Methodist Church, 1886

Campbell Street Methodist Church South, constructed 1887-88

The growth of Springfield, the growth of St. Paul's Methodist Church and the leadership of Pastor W.B. Palmore created the opportunity for a second Methodist Church in Springfield. Land had been purchased at the corner of Division Street and Campbell Avenue. The new church was established in 1886, with thirteen charter members and Pastor W.W. Jared. A year later, ground was broken for a new building on the site. In April 1888, a large, one-room, red-brick church was dedicated. The cost of the facility was an estimated $6,500. Originally named Palmore Chapel, it was changed at Dr. Palmore's request to Campbell Street Methodist Church.

Over the next several decades, church growth necessitated plans for additonal space. A pledge campaign began in the fall of 1920. Construction of the $30,000 education building was completed in December 1922. The second floor was used for worship services until the new sanctuary could be built for what was now over 330 attendees. Needing to allow the building fund to grow, it was in June 1927, that the cornerstone for the new sanctuary was laid. The $52,000 sanctuary was completed in December 1927. Debt payments on the loan become very difficult from 1931 through 1934, during the Depression years. After some financial recovery, efforts were made to eliminate the loan, with a mortgage burning on Sunday, November 25, 1945.

Campbell Street Methodist Church South, 1950s

In the 1950s, the sanctuary was updated with air conditioning and a new heating sytem. Anticipating future growth, additional properties to the west were purchased. The Springfield City Council also designated all city streets running east to west to be known as streets. All north to south streets were to be known as avenues. The church was now named the Campbell Avenue Methodist Church. In 1967, an additional education building was added and extensive remodeling allowed for the growing membership. In 1968, a national merger of the United Brethren Church and the Methodist Church necessitated another name to change, to Campbell Avenue United Methodist Church.

Adjacent house properties were purchased in the 1970s for additonal parking and a new parsonage. A new thrift center was created for the women's rummage sales. On May 18, 1982, the church was placed on the Registry of Historic Buildings by the Historic Sites Board of Springfield and Greene County.

It was determined that the residential areas of Springfield were now located in the southern section of the city. The church was being surrounded by commercial properties. In 1984, the membership voted to sell its properties to the General Council of the Assemblies of God. Later that year, a 10-acre plot of ground was found and purchased at 1747 E. Republic Road. Temporary services were held in the nearby Cumberland Presbyterian Church. The first services were held in the new building on December 15, 1985. The decision to move and rebuild was difficult for many of the members who harbored bad feelings, but many new members had been added, along with a growing number of educational and ministry-related organizations.

Current Information

3555 South Fremont Avenue
(417) 887-0600
www.campbellumc.org/history

Resources Used

75th Anniversary booklet
100 Years, 1886-1986, centennial booklet
www.campbellumc.org/history

Campbell Street Methodist Church South, 2017

South Street Christian Church, 1886

South Street Christian Church

South Street Christian Church grew out of the Springfield Christian Church over division concerning the use of musical instruments in the church. In 1886, Rev. E.G. Laughlin led about eighty members to organize the South Street Christian Church. The group met temporarily in the Mansfield Opera House until a new facility was constructed in 1887, on the corner of South and Elm Streets. Organizations were established for education, ministry and missions work, as well as raising funds for church needs. Within one year the church membership had doubled to over 160.

The church maintained a rather strict "code of Christian conduct." It was reported that…

> *The church board removed a sister deemed 'unworthy of membership' because she failed to heed the call to "reform her ways." They also denied a letter of transfer until a couple who danced and played cards should apologize and mend their ways. The church janitor once had fifty cents deducted from his salary for forgetting to turn off the gas one night. And in 1901, church officers were delegated to sit under the gallery, among the young people, to maintain order.*

The church continued its dramatic growth and bought an adjoining lot in anticipation of a new building. By 1908, a membership list

South Street Christian Church, South Avenue at Elm

recorded 889 members. Pledge drives found the membership faithful and committed. On October 10, 1910, a new sanctuary costing $40,000 was dedicated. A new pipe organ was also added to the sanctuary.

Under very capable pastoral leadership, the church became active in community needs. It established a School of the Bible at Drury College, conducted several successful interdenominational city-wide revival services, and offered its facilities as an emergency hospital during the widespread influenza epidemic in 1918. Such community activities helped to increase the church membership. By 1919, the church had more than 1,000 members. By 1927, church membership had reached 1,743. During this time, the First Christian Church of Springfield reunited with South Street, using the South Street facilities. New organizations within the church increased its educational and ministry efforts within its membership.

The tremendous growth and outreach was halted during the stressful Depression era of the 1930s. Selling of some church properties, across-the-board cuts in staff salaries, and closing the church doors three days a week helped to keep the church afloat. Even with these cost-saving efforts, ministry and mission work continued. Financial help was given to the Forest Hills Christian Church in relocating to Walnut Street with a new building.

The experiences of World War II brought emphasis on the purchase of war bonds and the loss of young men in the service of the country. Women took many places of leadership in the church with the absence of the men to the war effort. After the war, women continued to play important roles within the church as staff members and eventually as elders. A growing number of church members also were ordained as ministers. The pastor, Dr. William Gibble commented, "South Street has certainly produced more ministers than it has used up!"

In the next few decades, a new emphasis was placed on assisting and starting new church works, the National Avenue Christian Church and Brentwood Christian Church. The church also became a major supporter of new community ministry efforts, such as Crosslines and Meals-on-Wheels. The church facilities were once again pushing capacity limits. A new church sanctuary was completed in March 1972. A new educational building was added in 1986.

Current Information

500 South South Avenue
(417) 862-7079
www.southstreetchristian.org/site/

Resources Used

"Death of an Edifice," *Springfield Leader-Press*, February 13, 1917, page 2

Fairbanks and Tuck, *Past and Present Greene County, Missouri,* 1915

The First One Hundred Years, 1886-1986, centennial booklet

www.southstreetchristian.org/site/

South Street Christian Church, 2017

Macedonia Baptist Church, 1886

Macedonia Baptist Church was organized in 1886 in the Old Rose School House. It was located north of the present building across Sunshine Road, behind the Highway Patrol station. No records are available.

In 1910, the church was called Macedonia Missionary Baptist Church. In 1912, the church was called Macedonia Baptist Church. The church then moved to a new building (no date available) located at 4000 Sunshine Road. Worship services were held once a month, on the second Sunday (sometimes at 11:00 a.m. or at 3:00 p.m.). The pastors were paid $50.00 per year. At times this was in the form of farm products.

The church disbanded between 1918 and 1923, but was reorganized in 1923. During the time the church was disbanded, Mary Owens taught Sunday School and Baptist Young People's Union every Sunday.

In September of 1950, with the help of church members and sister churches, the church built its educational building. Temple Baptist Church deeded the property to the church for this building. Fred Plank was pastor when it was dedicated on October 28, 1951.

In February of 1958, under the leadership of John Wright, ground was broken for the foundation of the sanctuary. The architect was Earnest Ward. Construction was by Pete Durham, with the help of the membership of the church. On September 28, 1958, the new building was dedicated and the cornerstone laid. The names of all members of the church and important dates and happenings were put in a metal box that

Macedonia Baptist Church, 1984

Macedonia Baptist Church, 2017

was then sealed in the cornerstone. H.H. McGinty was the dedicatorial speaker. December 7, 1958, their first worship services were held in the new sanctuary, which is now the gym and fellowship hall.

On August 20, 1961, Reverend Charles H. Hufft was called by the church to be the pastor. He accepted and delivered his first sermon as pastor on September 24, 1961. Also, in October, 1961, the first minister of music, Charles Anderson, was hired. Darrell Hinds, Young Harper, Art Morris and Jon Glenn were also music directors. The first music committee was appointed in August 1957. Carl McCroskey served as chairman. Carl McCaully was appointed music director, but refused to be paid for it. Under the leadership of Reverend Hufft, a church library was organized in January 1962. The Brotherhood was organized September 16, 1962. No date is available on the organization of the Women's Missionary Union.

In April 1963, ground was broken and the first unit of the new educational building was started. Construction was by Luther Essary, and Warren and Goodin were the architects. Dedication services for this unit were held on September 29, 1963. The speaker was Dr. Earl Harding, executive director for the Missouri Baptist Convention. In June 1964, the interior of the old education building was destroyed by fire. Classes were held outside until the building was rebuilt.

In February 1965, the church voted to purchase property facing Sunshine Street at a cost of $38,500.00. Also at this meeting, the church approved the purchase of 5.5 acres of ground on South Golden for a price of $6,000.00. It was to be used as a future mission site. On August 15, 1965, the church approved the purchase of property at the 3000 block of West Sunshine Street (Woodside Supply). The cost was $19,500.00. These purchases were all financed with the sale of church bonds from the ABC Bonding Company.

In April 1966, the second unit of the new educational building was started. The first classes were held in this unit August 7, 1966. The new unit was dedicated September 11, 1966. The speaker was former pastor, Rev. John B. Wright.

The names of the pastors which have served the church, for which there are records, are:

1910 to 1913	H.C. Cunningham
1914 to 1915	Reverend Foley
1915 to 1916	T.M. Savage
1917 to 1918	John Killian
	Reverend Forshee
	John Rhaiff
1924 to 1925	Marvin Crocker
1926 to 1927	John Youngblood
1927 to 1929	Ross Carter
1930	Rolla Cook
1931	Tom Martin
1932	Reverend Tucker
1933 to 1935	Melvin Womack
1936 to 1937	Ross Carter (second time)
1937 to 1938	Luther Rogers (full time)
1939 to 1940	Thomas Miles (Chaplin at Medical Center)
1941 to 1948	(Church inactive part of time - no records available)
1949 to 1953	Fred Plank
1953 to 1954	Jack Rowley
1954 to 1961	John B. Wright
1961 to 1975	Charles H. Hufft
1975 to 1976	Charles Draper
1977 to 1982	Ron Lilly

1982 to 2001	Charles H. Hufft (second time)
2001 to 2004	Mike Miller
2004 to 2005	David Carpenter
2005 to 2006	Jim Wilcox (transitional pastor)
2006 to 2007	Jim Carter
2007 to present	Rich Jenkins

Current Information

3110 West Sunshine Street
(417) 882-6647
www.macedoniabc.com/about-us/

Resources Used

Bartee, Wayne C., *Greene County Baptist Churches in Ministry, 1838-1984*

Fairbanks and Tuck, *Past and Present Greene County, Missouri*, 1915

Materials provided from the church office

Moser, Arthur Paul, *Churches of Greene County, MO*, 1983

www.macedoniabc.com/about-us/

St. John's (German) Evangelical Church, 1887 St. John's United Church of Christ, 1957

The original church and parsonage of St. John's United Church of Christ

The large influx of immigrants settling in and around Springfield, Missouri, found the need for community, maintaining tradition, and assimilation. A good number of these people had migrated to the United States from Germany. Although several other traditional denominations were able to provide religious assimilation for some of the immigrants, there still remained a number of German evangelicals who were not comfortable in other denominational practices.

The first effort to gather these German evangelicals was made by the Evangelical Church at Billings, Missouri, in 1887. The ministers of the church, Reverends Baltzer and Walzer, worked for the first meeting of the evangelicals in Springfield. It was reported in the *Springfield Daily Herald*, September 17, 1887, that the group met at 4:00 p.m. in the St. Paul's United Methodist Church on the corner of Walnut and South Streets. The first service was held and the main Scripture was from Ephesians 3:13-21 with the topic, "The Periscope of the Church." Five children of various ages received Holy Baptism. They sang three "suitable songs of Mozart and the Chapel Schtzgerst Sandag Song."

At this same time in St. Louis, Charles Gorges had been unable to attend the first meeting in Springfield. He met with Reverend R. Agricola and shared the need for a fulltime minister for the group in Springfield. The minister agreed to come to Springfield and investigate the situation. He felt impressed to serve the new group. After agreeing to become a member of the Synod, he became St. John's first minister.

He quickly contacted the German families and invited them to an informal conference concerning the possible organization of the church. The group met in the German Free Scholl Society Hall, in the Kirby Arcade, on the southwest corner of the Springfield square. A short time later, October 17, 1887, a second meeting was held at the Cumberland Presbyterian Church on the corner of Jefferson Avenue and Olive Street. A constitution for the church was read and the council was elected. The church was now organized with approved leaders and guidelines for operation.

A more permanent location for the church was desired. The group first met in a residence on the south side of Nichols Street, east of Main Street. They would convene there for about a year and a half while the nearby church hall was erected. In 1906, the new church building was built at the corner of Scott and Main Streets (current location). It cost $2,600.

In 1924, a new addition to the church was built at a cost of $7,000. The Geneva Pipe organ was installed in June 1937. The old church hall was torn down in 1948 to make way for the parish hall. In 1983, the church was recognized as a historic site.

In 1957, the church joined with the United Church of Christ. The denomination is actually a combination of four other denominations: Reformed, founded by Zwingli; Evangelical; Congregational, founded by Robert Browne; and Christian. The Congregational and Christian churches joined in 1931. The Evangelical and Reformed churches united on June 26, 1934. The two new groups merged on June 25, 1957, forming the United Church of Christ.

From its beginning, and for the first thirty-three years, German was the only language used in the church services, Sunday School, Confirmation and the German School. By 1920, it was becoming apparent that German was no longer being taught in the home. Reverend F. Kemme noticed the decline in attendance, largely because of the common disuse of the German language. He introduced the use of the English language in all of the services.

A 1960 study indicated the need for another United Church of Christ in Springfield, Missouri. Property was purchased in September of that year, on South Fremont Avenue. The Chapel of St. John's United Church of Christ was dedicated on September 19, 1971. It began to outgrow its facilities and construction was started for a new sanctuary. It was dedicated on October 14, 1984. The two churches are now separate congregations offering assistance to each other.

For the original congregation, a declining neighborhood and limited pastoral assistance has led to a decline in membership and attendance. A small, but faithful, congregation continues the traditions of this historic church.

St. John's Church, Scott and Main streets

Current Information

1110 North Main Street
(417) 862-8161
www.stjohnsuccscottandmain.org/about

Resources Used

Fairbanks and Tuck, *Past and Present Greene County, Missouri,* 1915
St. John's Centennial, 1887-1987, booklet
Written materials provided by a church member
www.stjohnsuccscottandmain.org/about

St. John's United Church of Christ, 2017

Third Baptist Church, 1889
East Avenue Baptist Church, 1890
National Heights Baptist Church, 1979

The efforts of many in this congregation make a wonderfully rich historical view in the publication written for their centennial on July 29, 1989. The history gives a challenge to new generations to record events for the future. The membership, at the time of the centennial, stood at 808, with many of the members from third and fourth generation families.

To get a clear view of this church, one should look at the city of Springfield around the year 1890. It was a time of prosperity. The railroad had extended south from Kansas City and as it flourished, so did the city. Workers moved to the city to fill the jobs the railroad required. The pastors of the First Baptist Church and Robberson Avenue agreed that a new church could be needed. W.C. Armstrong, an ordained minister and a graduate of Southwest Baptist College, canvassed the area at their request. After two months, they found that a church was needed.

On the evening of July 28, 1889, an open-air service was called and, the next evening, a council was called. They met in an oak grove at the northwest corner of Dale Street and Springfield Avenue, now National Avenue. The express purpose was to organize a church. Some 40 people, as well as delegates from First Baptist Church, attended the second meeting. At the conclusion, 16 came forward as charter members. The Articles of Faith and the Covenant were read, and the church was constituted under the name Third Baptist Church, with W.C. Armstrong as the first pastor.

Meetings continued in the oak grove, but as the days began to shorten, the weather made shelter a priority. A plot was purchased on East Avenue, just south of Turner Street, as a site for a building. The price of the property is not known, but speculation puts the price at around $750.00. The church rented Koehler Hall, which served as the meeting place throughout the winter. A frame building with a modest bell tower was erected on the East Avenue property. To curb cost, members did most of the building. Some technical labor and materials were paid with outside financing. While awaiting completion of the building, Third Avenue Baptist was admitted to the Greene County Baptist Association, as the 32nd Baptist Church in the county. The name of the church was changed, sometime in 1890, to East Avenue Baptist Church to reflect its location. It continued under that name until 1979, when the congregation adopted the change to National Heights Baptist Church, after moving to its current location.

East Avenue Baptist Church

In 1890, a Sunday School for all ages and a ladies aid was organized for prayer meetings and to raise money for church expenses. Membership had grown to 60 around the time the East Avenue building was first in use. The function of the church was to provide a place of worship for those families who worked for the Frisco Railroad.

Several pastors served at the church in the very early years and, in June of 1891, a supply pastor came to the church who received aid from the state board to pay his monthly salary. The church continued to meet without a full time pastor, but a vote in October 1891 was passed to call a full time pastor at $500.00 per year. No action was taken on this vote since, in December, they accepted E.T. Sloan to preach two Sundays a month at a yearly salary of $265.00. In February, he came to the church as a full time pastor at the salary of $25.00 per month.

Some items of decorum were noted during Pastor Sloan's tenure. A resolution prohibiting its members from dancing, card playing, or use of intoxicating drinks was drafted in August of 1892. Another was added in February of 1895 against unscriptural marriages. Their belief was that the Bible allowed only one cause for separation in marriage. Divorce had become prevalent, and this was a request for members to govern themselves. (A note in this historical record states that committees of one were appointed to investigate rumors against members not conforming to Christian standards.)

Like most churches in their infancy, finances created the largest obstacle to growth. In September of 1896, the church's expenses were $1.60, but only $1.58 was collected leaving a deficit of 2 cents. It is also noted the pastor's salary was in arrears by $45.35.

Several pastors came and went from the church until 1901, when E.T. Sloan, after having left in August of 1887, came back to the church and a congregation of 213 members.

The membership voted in 1901, that each member would financially support the church every six months or charges would be brought against him or her for violating a church covenant. Committees were appointed to counsel members for infractions of nonattendance, social sins, disorderly walk, and, of course, nonpayment.

During the early 1900s, a depression again gripped the nation, and many jobs were lost. Pay for work was meager, with a common laborer earning 60 cents to a dollar a day for 10 to 12 hours of work. A carpenter could earn as much as $2.00 a day. Cash flow deficits for the church were inevitable, and pastors from many churches found it necessary to seek other work to support their families.

The church building was aging and needed a new roof, windows and doors. Expansion to accommodate membership growth was also needed. Lots, one on the north and one on the south of the building, were acquired to allow for the growing membership. The enlargement on the two lots was completed with funds borrowed for the project, as well as repair to the church's furnace. A pressing need was for a baptistry. Baptisms were still performed in Doling Park Lake. The cost was estimated at $30.00, but when completed, the actual cost was $58.64.

Finances for the church continued to be a burden. Getting members to hold up their financial obligation was a continuing battle. In May of 1907, it was decided if delinquency continued for three months, it would be investigated to determine if there was a valid reason. In December of 1908, expenses totaled $99.45 but only $62.75 had been collected. Among expenses listed for the month was a new broom at a cost of 75 cents.

Throughout its life, the church had pastors who came and stayed for short durations, serving at the whim of the congregation, unless they themselves resigned. They were called for one year, subject to reelection, or the pastors would leave without providing notice meaning the church was often without leadership. In November 1910, a vote for an indefinite call to pastors was effected immediately. This required the church, or the pastor, to give notice two months prior to resignation or dismissal.

In May of 1910, Brother N.J. Breshears engaged the church in a series of tent meetings. At that time, the church endorsed alliance with the Missionary Society, as well as with Greene County Missionary Union. Also, a Baptist Young Peoples Union was organized.

The bell in the church tower was purchased in 1890, and taken down in August of 1910, to be used at a tent meeting on the corner of Commercial Street and Springfield Avenue. The bell was rehung only to fall and suffer a crack during the fire in the church in 1912.

During the winter of 1909-1910, an evangelist, E.P. Sitton, conducted a revival and 150 decisions were made for the church. The church invited D.C. Barb, district missionary, to participate. This culminated with him being called to serve the church under the new directive for pastors. Although pastoring the church, he was not ordained. However, he was given power to select a council and invite all Baptist churches to send their pastors, elders, and deacons for the purpose of his ordination. This was accomplished on May 12, 1912.

In February of 1912, the church voted to purchase gasoline lighting at a cost of $34.60. A down payment of $8.65 was made and an amount was paid monthly. In April, an attempt to meet obligations in a more orderly fashion was necessary, as funds in the treasury were still frequently falling short.

On August 21, 1912, the church building burned to the ground. Originally, it was declared that fire by lightning was the cause. No evidence or allegations were made or found to dispute the claim, but as late as June 1939, the words "struck by lightning" were deleted from the historical record and the words "completely destroyed by fire", with no explanation as to the cause, was used instead. In a news account, the building was valued at $5,000.00, but was insured for only $1,500.00.

Sunday School convened August 25th in the grove across the street from the burned building. Plans for rebuilding were discussed and an interim meeting place would be needed. Reverend Barb's messages, both morning and evening of that Sunday, would be the crisis of East Avenue Church. Now a congregation of 500, with a Sunday School of 250, was without a church home. At meetings held in the grove, a committee was appointed to submit plans for a new church of fireproof materials, with a capacity to seat 800. Another committee was given the task of raising the funds that would be needed, while the task of disposing of the rubbish from the fire was given to the trustees. The strongest foundation of the church was the workers who had a vision to rebuild.

East Avenue Baptist Church after the fire in August 1912

All necessary work of the church continued in spite of not having a building, as plans for a new building moved forward. The committee was given the authority to employ an architect for a building 50'X 50'with a basement. Bids for the work were sought at once.

As would be expected, plans did not move forward without dissention among those making the decisions. Several members, after pledging financially to help construct the church, rescinded their offers and left the church. Reverend Barb also tendered his resignation. The church reverted to their rule of allowing a pastor to stay with the church for one year, then needing to be reelected.

A contract was awarded to Mr. James Milliken for the completion of the basement, at a cost of $1,389.00. The work was expected to be done by Christmas of 1912. Committees were elected to take care of essential items such as seating, heating and lights, so the basement could be used. The date for completion was missed by a few weeks, as the first service was held in the basement on January 13, 1913, warmed by a stove donated by the builder, James Milliken.

Impatient for the church structure to be completed, work immediately began on the rest of the building. A plea went out to all the Baptist churches in the state asking for assistance in paying for the project. No reports of assistance were recorded, but the work began in April, 1913. A pulpit committee had been appointed, and Reverend C.E. Calvert was voted in as of March 28, 1913.

Construction completion was not met until May 7. Soliciting for the work began, but a contract would not be signed until the treasury showed $1,500.00 in the building fund. Once again, the members were admonished for neglecting their contributions to the church. At the dawn of 1914, a frenzy of activity to complete the new building was underway, as a meeting was held to plan the celebration of the 25th anniversary of the church in July.

Finances continued to be a problem. A committee of 12 was appointed to install a plan known as "The Every Member Canvass System." The members were directed to borrow the funds to pay off the indebtedness on the building, including selling all materials left after construction. The bell was entrusted to the care of Brother C.S. Riddlesperger, who was to place it where he felt it appropriate. It was decided by this committee that the two front windows of the church would be made of stained glass.

At the final meeting of the silver anniversary year, the church voted to send the pastor out to solicit the funds needed for the building. How this would be accomplished was left to his judgment and his expenses would be paid out of his collections.

In early 1916, confessions by church members of misadventures resulted in forgiveness. A series of "thou shall not" activities was adopted and reviewed by members. Those prohibited activities included dancing, card playing, games of chance, gambling, and the use of intoxicants.

In July, a new bell was presented by O.C. Mitchell to replace the one which had been cracked in the fire of 1912. He stipulated that the bell not be rung when the church was in debt.

In February 1917, Reverend Calvert was released as pastor after having served the church since March of 1913. In April, the pulpit committee voted unanimously to the election of J.G. Barnes. Barnes was pleased to accept as he had family close to Springfield.

The United States declared war on Germany on April 6, 1917, and the first U.S. Troops landed in France on June 26, 1917. December 7, 1917, President Wilson declared war on Austria. Many of the young men from the church served. Church was a happier place during the years of the Reverend Barnes' pastorate, except for the nation being ravaged by war. A revival planned for September 1918, was cancelled by mayoral proclamation. No public meetings could be held, except those necessary to the war effort, to prevent the further spread of influenza, which gripped the city. During this time, while many troops died in battle, citizens at home were dying of this disease, which reached epidemic proportions and forced the closure of schools.

Little business for the church took place during the period of 1919 and 1920, as the nation adjusted to the signing of the armistice of November 11, 1918.

Women's Missionary Society was very active during this time. The women prepared lunches and carried them six blocks to the railroad workers each day. The lunches contained fried chicken, vegetables, dessert and a hot roll at a cost of 35 cents. The funds did much to promote foreign and home mission activity.

In January of 1922, a strike of great proportions affected the members of the church. The strike was against the St. Louis-San Francisco Railroad, (Frisco). The strike created warring factions, those who supported the strike and those against. Tempers flared and meetings at the church were, at times, turned into a battlefront. The heads of households needed to feed their families, and some crossed the picket lines and worked during the strike. That created deep resentment.

During this sad time for the church, Reverend Barnes offered his resignation. A vote was declared that any pastor elected would require a three-fourths majority with a quorum of 25, but this was changed to 15. Newt N. Smelsor was elected in April. Brother Smelsor was not recalled at the end of his second year and left the church June 1, 1925. During a special meeting, Elder Earl W. French was unanimously elected in September of 1925. Brother French served this congregation for 18 years. This longevity had never been enjoyed by the church. He resigned in February of 1942, to accept a position as missionary to the Greene-Webster County Association. He was missed and much loved by the church members.

Early in Reverend French's pastorate, additional classrooms for Sunday School were needed. A committee appointed to investigate the new classrooms inspected used brick being removed from Commercial Street, which was being repaved. If suitable, 20,000 bricks would be purchased for the addition. The bricks were purchased and work on the addition began March of 1927, the 38th anniversary of the church.

Early in 1929, the church kitchen was remodeled under the supervision of the women of the congregation. That same year, the pastor was granted a three-week vacation with pay and the insurance on the building was increased to $10,000.00.

The stock market crash of 1929, threw the nation into a weakened economic condition. Through the sale of eggs collected from the congregation, the church was able to support an old folks home in Ironton, Missouri. Fundraising efforts were started for the installation of a new furnace in the church.

In July of 1931, the treasurer's report showed a balance for the month of $34.53. The church was showing some financial stability, and the budget set at year's end for 1932 was $4,670.00.

Membership continued to increase during the years of the Depression, creating other needs for the church. A new Sunday School and baptistry building fund was started in February of 1936, with a goal to raise $1,000.00 before the church's anniversary. The addition would contain a basement and one story, and would be built to the west of the main auditorium. Dedication of the project was celebrated on October 10, 1937. Vacation Bible School was started for the first time that year as well, with an enrollment of 205 and consistent attendance of 171.

Franklin Roosevelt was president when the church celebrated its 50th anniversary in 1939. The occasion was observed with a pageant, followed by the morning service and a basket dinner served in the basement. The evening service was a presentation of a cantata, "The Message Eternal," by the sanctuary choir.

On December 7, 1941, Japan attacked the battleships stationed at Pearl Harbor and the nation was again at war. Many hours of service were lent to the war effort, but nothing could compare to the lives of two of their own lost in the battles. Forty-four young men from East Avenue Baptist served their country during the conflict.

The church, in an effort to publicize and evangelize to the community, began a 15- minute, 3-day a week radio program in 1945.

After a period of interim and short-term leadership in the church, Reverend L.D. Eppinette was elected December 5, 1945. During his pastorate, a mission church was established. It was begun with Sunday School at Grandview School, northeast of town. In January 1957, it celebrated its first pastor and became full time. A bid was made on Grandview property and financing was secured for the purchase. The mission would make payments to the extent of its ability and East Avenue would pay the remaining balance. Unfortunately, staffing became difficult , and the mission fell by the wayside.

During 1953, when Reverend Eppinette had been with the church for seven years, a split over his leadership and duties rocked the congregation. Some felt that he was frequently unavailable to attend to the business and activities of the church and wanted him dismissed. After much discussion and interviews, it was decided that the reverend spent too much time on extracurricular activities, namely the practice

East Avenue Baptist Church, ca. 1950

of magic for profit. It was also reported that he was in favor of local options to repeal prohibition.

After Reverend Eppinette's ouster, Reverend E.F. Maness was called. He did much to calm the tempers and aid the healing process in the church after the tenure of the former pastor. Brother Maness had served for less than two years when Brother Eugene Grubbs was elected. The membership had grown to 565 active members with an average of 710 at Sunday School.

Brother Grubbs supported a building fund drive to add an education building to the church. The goal was high - $100,000.00. Some said it couldn't be done, but by the end of the campaign, over $85,000.00 was pledged and the education building was completed at a cost of $109,000.00.

Brother Grubbs' stay was short and Brother Maness stepped back in until the pulpit committee finished the work of finding a new pastor. One extremely hot and uncomfortable Sunday morning in August as Brother Maness was at the pulpit, he was discouraged as he looked out at the sleepy, drowsy and uncomfortable congregation. Pulpit thumping and a raised voice did little to rouse the congregation from their malaise of heat and discomfort. With a chuckle, Brother Maness closed his Bible and strode firmly from the pulpit as he told the assembled crowd "You are dismissed. If you are not interested, neither am I."

Reverend Jim E. Jefferies came to the church in August of 1965. His tenure would last almost a quarter of a century. The church celebrated their 85th anniversary exactly 10 years to the day that Reverend Jefferies came to lead the church. Most congregants lived within walking distance or a short drive to the church, but now it was becoming necessary to implement a means of gathering those from remote areas to the church as the neighborhood began to expand. A transportation plan was enacted, making it possible to purchase a bus and the necessary license and insurance.

It was becoming apparent that the area around the church was now dominated with the establishment of a Bible College. Small residences were the norm in the neighborhood, and now, most were turned into student rentals. The area had a transient atmosphere, which would hamper the continued growth of the church. A long range planning committee was put into place to explore a solution. An attorney represented the church in a rezoning project to allow the sale of the church property to be used for endeavors other than a church. Property was available to the south of the church but the vote for its purchase failed. Several parcels of land were under consideration by the church. The most desirable was 13 acres north of Interstate 44 at National and Norton. The owner of the property was offered $45,000.00, but no less than $65,000.00 would be accepted. Other properties were considered but fell short of what was desired. The owner of the property at National and Norton was approached and offered $40,000.00 for eight of the 13 acres. Thus, the 8 acres were acquired and plans to develop them began.

The property could be used for relocation of the church, or as a mission point. A motion to wait six months and perhaps sell the National property if the East Avenue property was not sold was dismissed. A contract was agreed upon with Hood-Rich Architects, at a fee of $14,000.00, for the design of a new building. There was debate about the moral obligation to the founders of the church over selling the East Avenue property, but after examination of the deeds by an attorney it was determined the property could be sold and the proceeds used for the same purpose without conflict with church doctrine.

A contractual agreement to sell the East Avenue property was signed with Baptist Bible College, but the transaction fell through after plans for the National property were well on their way. Accordingly, the college agreement was discharged, and the obligation was cancelled.

By August of 1977, the final approval was given to relocate to North National. A fundraising plan was needed with a goal of $200,000.00.

East Avenue Baptist Church, 1984

Levels to raise the funds were set in the following manner: $100,000.00, "Victory"; $150,000.00, "Praise the Lord"; $200,000.00, "Hallelujah." The campaign was aptly called "Stepping Forward on Faith."

Financing assurances from Empire Bank would make the new church home a reality, and so, on December 4, 1977, ground was broken. The members traveled to the new property, many of them armed with shovels. They gathered around the previously staked outline of the new building and while singing songs of faith, dedication and asking for God's blessing, the shovels dug into the earth and a new church building was given birth. Ultimately, the remaining five acres of land were acquired by the church. The final negotiated cost of construction of the building was $556,944.00.

By November of 1978, great progress was being made at the new site, now called National Heights Baptist Church. Votes for other names had been considered, but ultimately the vote favored National Heights Baptist Church.

Still the East Avenue site and other properties needed to be addressed. A sister church, Northwest Baptist, who sustained a total loss due to fire, considered several options then made an offer on the East Avenue property. It was accepted by mutual agreement of both congregations.

The last Sunday in April 1979, was named "Heritage Day," and celebrations were geared towards the remembrance of the East Avenue

Church and the future of National Heights. May 6, 1979, the first services in the new facility were planned, but not without some major adjustments, since the sanctuary was not complete. A crowd of 227 worshiped the first Sunday in the new home.

A new organ was sought after it was determined the organ at East Avenue could not be moved to National Heights. There was disagreement over the type of instrument, pipe or electric, however, it was felt that a pipe organ would better fit the new building. Then, of course, there was the expense. The price of the instrument would be $87,000.00, and a loyal and faithful anonymous member challenged the congregation to raise the money. If they would raise $77,000.00, the member would then pay the final $10,000.00 necessary for the purchase.

When the centennial year approached, it was decided that the whole year would be dedicated to the celebration. A wonderful surprise made the centennial an even bigger celebration when the church received a total bequest of $381,000.00 from the estate of Mr. Lyell F. Jones. This fulfilled the plan the church had of being debt free by its centennial anniversary. The church was 100 years old but still growing, and there were needs for the church family and the community. The bequest would help to make plans for continued growth a reality.

Many in the church were honored for their contributions in the service of the church during the centennial celebration. A dream session in April drew a good crowd ready to listen to and offer their ideas for where the church should go in the future. In May, the teachers and adult leaders were honored, with the children participating in Bible drills. A senior in high school, Shane Cobban, preached the sermon giving the church a glimpse of what the future held from its youth. In June, the church gave recognition to all who had left the church to pursue Christian ministries in other churches, both locally and throughout the country.

July 23, 2008, was a day of praise and celebration. Special invitations to former members and publicity in the press swelled attendance in excess of 500. Forty-five of those in attendance were recognized for 50 or more years of membership, and they were each presented with a long-stemmed, red rose. Thirteen with 40 or more years of membership were also in the crowded church. The centennial celebration gave the church the opportunity to recognize the retirement of the debt on the property with a ceremonial note burning. In addition, the church was still looking to the future when five acres north of the property was bought for $40,000.00, with plans to put it to use for a children's building and a Christian activity center.

The centennial marked the end of an era, but also a new beginning with promise for the future. In a conversation with the current pastor, Vaughn Weatherford, via email, he wrote that the building and activity center was completed as of 1991. When asked what he saw for the bicentennial of the church, he responded that, though he could not see that far ahead, he knew the church would continue to carry on its mission to share the gospel of Christ with the community and the world. It is the desire and prayer of the church to love God, love people and grow together.

There are no lofty goals for this church, just realistic desires to build and grow in love and commitment to the church family and the community. Considering the records of their history, they will continue and not only prosper, but flourish.

Current Information

3050 North National, 65803
(417) 833-4111
www.nationalheights.org

References

Bartee, Wayne. *Greene County Baptist Churches in Ministry, 1838-1984*

On This Rock – a History of National Heights Baptist Church – Nina Barclay Beatie

National Heights Baptist Church, 2017

Boulevard Methodist Church, 1889 Mount Carmel United Methodist Church, 1920

We had hoped to include more information about this church. Yet, after repeated contact attempts, the church has not responded to our requests for information on their organizational history. We have found some limited information from secondary sources that we have included.

In the late 1880s, mission-minded, concerned members of the Grace Methodist Church began Sunday School classes in their homes. When the classes became too large for the homes, a tent was erected in a nearby field. In 1889, a permanent structure was completed on land near Scott and Boulevard (National) Streets. The church was chartered with ten members under the pastoral care of Reverend Leckliter. Numerous families from Grace Methodist Church were involved in the building construction and organization. Originally, the church was referred to as the Boulevard Methodist Church.

In 1920, Mr. and Mrs. W.I. Bodine donated two lots on the corner of Bailey (Pythian) and Boulevard (National) Streets. A brick building was constructed in 1921, and the growing congregation moved into the new building. The name was then changed to Mount Carmel Methodist Church. Twenty years later the mortgage note was burned in special worship services.

Mount Carmel United Methodist Church, 2017

In 1973, a new education building was added for additional classrooms. The old sanctuary underwent extensive remodeling. Over the years, donated stained glass windows have been added to the sanctuary.

Current Information

1001 North National Avenue
(417) 866-7039
www.moumethodist.org/churchdetail/697668

Resources Used

Fairbanks and Tuck, *Past and Present Greene County, Missouri*, 1915
www.moumethodist.org/churchdetail/697668

Washington Avenue Church, 1889
Central Christian
Disciples of Christ, 1902

A reference in the forward written for the 125th anniversary of the church history, acknowledges a lack of documented history of the church prior to 1927. After that date, record keeping was less than all inclusive, as not everyone charged with the duty deemed events important enough to note. This results in little chronological history of the church. Being able to pin down the formalization of the start of the church cannot be accomplished through bits and pieces of history. However, events that are noted point to a church that had great magnetism in the community. For its 125th anniversary in 2014, the church threw a party for the neighborhood. Everything from free haircuts, to fun attractions and activities for the children, played a part in the festivities. People responded as the estimate of the crowd gathered was well over 1,000.

Inside the church in the "history room," memorabilia rests in glass-front cabinets. Some of the relics on display are a cassock (or robe) worn by one of the early ministers, and a silver communion set once used by Alexander Campbell, a founder of the 19th Century Restoration Movement. These are visual reminders of the history and the people of the church, along with black and white photographs depicting events with large gatherings of people. All have meaning and show the pride of those who call this church home.

Central Christian began as a Sunday School prior to its organization as a church. A few resources give the names of those who were the first ministers of the church, but they disagree. Maybe all are correct, as one named minister was leading at the church while another was supervising the Sunday School. They were separate entities, and were known to have an adversarial relationship. The reference in *Past and Present for Greene County,* written in 1915, gives credit to O.A. Carr with the organization of the church on January 5, 1890, when the church was referred to as Washington Avenue Church. Carr, according to reports in the press, gave the sermon at the dedication in December of 1889, but he was not named as the organizer.

Sanctuary of the original Central Christian Church, 1910

Yet, another reference names H.J. Underwood as the first to the pulpit. He conducted services in or around 1888, in the Grand Army of the Republic (GAR) Hall on Commercial Street. This was reportedly a small group of 14 people and a Sunday School. Underwood also led services in the Benton Avenue Methodist Episcopal Church. In December of 1889, the group moved into a newly-dedicated meetinghouse on Division Street and Washington Avenue, which was the location of the church. A series of revivals conducted by Reverend Underwood significantly increased his following, but he left this group to form yet another Christian Church back at the GAR Hall. Sometime in 1890, a new leader stepped in, Dr. R. Watson.

Dr. Watson found the church had suffered difficulties of one kind or another and most of the 125 followers, gathered by Reverend Underwood, had deserted the church. He left the church after 1891, as a Springfield City Directory lists William S. Tucker as minister. The church, from whatever problems it suffered, seemed unable to support a minister and was frequently without one.

Another leader, Reverend William Harlow, came in 1902. He came by way of Kansas City and his stay at the church was short. However, the impact of his time at the church served to do away with restrictions on the deed for use of the building and implement the name change from Washington Avenue Church to Central Christian Church.

Matilda Weaver, who was the niece of Springfield founder, John Campbell, provided the lot and paid for the construction of the original church building in 1889. She was associated with the First Christian Church and the possible reason she helped to build the church was in an effort to bring more churches to the north of Springfield. The lot was purchased for the sum of $2,150.00 and the church was built and furnished at a cost of $11,000.00. It was given as a gift to the church with a stipulation in the deed that instrumental music not be permitted during worship. This condition was observed until early in the 20th Century when Reverend W.E. Harlow came to fill the pulpit in the church. A condition of his acceptance was that there would be instrumental music in the church. Attempts were made to move the congregation to another house of worship to allow instrumental music, but, in the end a compromise was met when, for a stipulated amount paid, an unconditional deed was issued. For his insistence that the deed be modified, his dynamic personality, and his ability to bring people to the church, he is sometimes referred to as the founder of the church. His stay was short, as he was gone from the church by 1903. However, as evidenced by his influence, the membership at the now Central Christian Church was at 223. This was the starting point of the membership outgrowing the space. Harlow went on to serve at the First Christian Church and, in 1906, was responsible for the early negotiation that led to the joining with South Street Church in 1919.

Some of the names and dates of those who served at the church are like other events, lost to time and history. Without a complete written record of events until 1927, the importance should be that the church prospered under the leadership of several ministers and the efforts made through evangelizing. Many were brought into the fold of the church and, at one time, it was thought that the membership topped 1,500 souls.

E.C. Sechler was one of those who stayed and helped cement the church into a grand institution. He came in September of 1920, and stayed for eleven years. He took an interest in his converts beyond the church doors by helping them find employment, which accounts for the large growth of the church during his time. Over the time of his service, the membership had grown to 1,200. He is credited with many accomplishments at the church, including unifying the church and the Sunday School, which, in the past, had disagreements that kept

Washington Avenue Church

them at odds. The idea of bringing the two together was a trial during the summer months, but the plan worked and the congregation voted for it to continue. He introduced the practice of Wednesday evening services and it continues. He worked hard for the church, and was there in the beginning as plans for the new building were being developed. His health failed, but the board retained him as an inactive minister for two years until his health improved. Harvey L. Humphrey, a student at Drury College, was then asked to serve as acting minister. This led to him being heavily engaged in the demolition of the old building and construction of the new. Demolition began in 1926, and Mr. A.T. Thompson had been hired to remove the old building and build the new one on a cost plus plan. The blueprints for the new church were drawn up by the firm of Hawkins-Abbott Architects, submitted and enthusiastically approved. Then the building was erected very much where it now stands, on the same lot as the old church. Original plans called for a basement under the building, but this was changed at Humphrey's suggestion and two stories were added to the building instead. Humphrey stayed on until Reverend Sechler's health enabled him to return to his duties and witness the dedication of the new building.

In June of 1945, shortly after the war, Reverend Roy Price Fields came to the church. He watched as the men came home from the war. He served as president of the City Missions Board of the Disciples of Christ Springfield, that led to the organization of Brentwood Christian Church. He ministered to 1,155 members in the church and he felt that his time was spent mostly dealing with peoples' tragedies. He served the church until 1958.

In 1948, a pipe organ was purchased for the church. After refurbishing several years ago, it still adequately fills the church's needs.

When Reverend Mike McGinnis came to the church in February of 1963, he had an optimistic faith in Central Christian Church. He was told he would be serving in the pulpit of a dying church, as many older downtown churches were gone. This was a time when the inner city churches all over the country, not just in Springfield, were losing members, as moving away from the city and into the suburbs was becoming increasingly popular. He changed that and filled the pews due to his often-humorous sermons. He reportedly visited every one of the 1,000 plus members to get close to the people and meet them in their environment. He stayed with the church the longest of any of the prior ministers, and the length of his stay shows in the growth and closeness of the congregation. His abilities went beyond the church and into the community, with his active role in religious, as well as secular, organizations. This included teaching a class of lay ministers who were to be licensed to serve in small churches. He was there to help the congregation celebrate their Diamond Jubilee, and was conferred honorary degrees of Doctor of Divinity from Drury College and Drury School of Religion. He retired in 1997, after devoting 35 years to the church.

Sunday School was the lifeblood of the church and much importance was placed on the number in attendance. The average attendance by 1908, was 262, which continued to grow, even as Reverend Errett Sechler called for the unification of the church and the Sunday School. Credit at Central goes to one man, Guy Cowden, superintendent of the school. He served in that capacity for twenty-five years and took the responsibility of providing trained teachers who had a prepared lesson for every class. He was successful for 1,300 Sundays. A Springfield school is named in his honor. Emphasis was placed on rewarding each child on Promotion Day, when their names were called in the sanctuary, and they received their certificates to the next highest grade in front of the congregation. Each class vied for the coveted honor of winning the banner awarded to the class with the highest attendance. Promotion Day eventually lost favor, and now a child is promoted to the next class on their

New building of Central Christian Church, dedicated in 1927

A baptizing at the James River

birthday, but no longer in the sanctuary as in years past. Attendance records began to slip as more churches were built and the move from the inner city became more common. The average in the 1940s and1950s was 380 to 400.

Central has kept pace with the changing theology of the Disciples of Christ, allowing some of the early practices to fall by the wayside. Discontinuation of baptism by the flow of water, as Jesus was baptized, met with some disappointment, as now an indoor baptistry is used. The change from the use of the common cup for communion has been abandoned. In addition, infant baptism and forbidding the use of musical instruments in the church have lost favor. Some of the practices have been replaced as having been too rigid or simply outdated. Central's close association with Drury College has kept practices in the church and the theological changes within the denomination current. Many of the personnel from the college are members, active in leadership and freely share their knowledge with the church.

Since the year 2000, concentrated efforts on making a difference in the neighborhoods surrounding the church has been Central Christian's major thrust. Shirley Musser, a lifelong member and director of visitation, saw a need. With the help of the local elementary school faculty and dedicated volunteers, she started an afternoon program called Culture Club. The idea was to help with homework and give some needed supervision to the children. The program has now grown into serving meals three days a week to children ranging from kindergarten to fifth grade. A sufficient number attend to make the program

Central Christian Church, 2017

a worthwhile effort. In 2014, the church budget showed $43,000.00 for community betterment. More residents from the surrounding neighborhoods began to occupy the pews. Currently, approximately 150 to 175 attend on any given Sunday. The history of this church is rich, and its contribution to the city of Springfield is far-reaching and positive. Thousands have walked through its doors. As it continues, the members will write the history, not only of the church, but also of the community.

Several times talk has centered on moving the church to the south to go where the growth and new communities are. In the end, all have agreed that the corner of Washington and Division is where this beacon of light has shown for many years, and so the church will stay in this neighborhood.

Current Information

1475 North Washington Avenue at Division Street
(417) 869-7241
www.ccspringfield.org/

Resources Used

Forward Through the Ages – A History of Central Christian Church – Garner J. Phillips Published by Central Christian Church

Past and Present of Greene County Missouri – Jonathan Fairbanks and Clyde Edwin Tuck thelibrary.org.- greenecountymo.gov/archives/Springfield

www.ccspringfield.org/

Chapter Five

1890s

Historical Notes

By 1899, Springfield's population had grown to 23,000. The town established "free public schools, a gas company which serviced some 100 gas street lamps, a telephone exchange with nearly 300 customers, a sewage system, a new hospital, a high school building, free mail delivery with a post office building, and a paid fire department." The town also acquired "several mills and light industries, the most famous being the Springfield Wagon Company which produced 6,000 wagons annually for a national market."

Churches Established No Longer Qualifying

Springfield Avenue Presbyterian Church, 1892

Temple Israel, 1890

Since the congregation has moved to Rogersville, technically, they no longer qualify in the required criteria. However, their long and distinguished service in Springfield's history must be recognized.

There is evidence of Jewish immigrants from eastern Europe in Springfield by 1890. Three years later, a synagogue was organized in the city. By 1900, the congregation had grown large enough to organize a second synagogue. Temple Israel aligned with the reformed Jewish movement, while the new group was more orthodox in nature. There was good cooperation between the two groups.

Between the wars, the national attitude of anti-Semitism had little impact within the local Jewish communities. They "quietly accepted the social constraints" at that time. In 1933, the orthodox group was able to build a modest synagogue. The two groups shared the facility during World War II. The orthodox group paid off the loan on the building and had enough resources to hire a part-time rabbi. A new social hall was constructed in 1952.

Many of the orthodox congregation were aging and dying. Orthodox Judaism had a hard time existing on its own in Springfield and joined forces with the reformed group. A resurgence of new Jewish families arrived in the 1970s from the East coast. This revitalized the congregation and a new suburban facility was built outside of Springfield in 1996, and renamed itself Temple Israel.

Current Information

5910 South Farm Road 193, Rogersville, MO 65742
(417) 888-5151
www.springfieldsynagogue.org

Churches Currently Operating

Grant Street Baptist Church, 1891
  Grant Avenue Baptist Church, 1950
Boulevard Baptist Church, 1891
  Pythian (Home) Baptist Church, 1912
    Just for Jesus Church, 2016
St. Joseph's Catholic Parish (Church), 1892
Ray Chapel Baptist Church, 1895
  Hamlin Memorial Baptist Church, 1908
Reorganized Latter Day Saints Church, 1896
  Community of Christ, Chapel of Peace, 2001
Seventh Day Adventist, 1899

Grant Street Baptist Church, 1891
Grant Avenue Baptist Church, 1950

In a publication prepared for the centennial of the church, the forward acknowledges that the history is not complete and will never be complete, but we do know this organization has weathered much since its beginning in 1891.

The first recorded information was May 13, 1888, when First Baptist Church, which had its beginnings in Springfield in 1852, organized a Sunday School. The school continued to grow in their first meeting place on Grant Street near Chestnut, under the wise leadership of its superintendent, W.D. Sheppard.

Grant Avenue Baptist was organized the first of two times on the evening of July 27, 1891, with members from several churches present. After the articles of Faith and the Church Covenant were read, a council was organized, with messengers from First Baptist, Robberson Avenue, and East Avenue Churches. The council recommended that a church be organized. The moderator gave invitations for new members and 31 were baptized, with an additional 58 coming from a revival meeting. With a membership of 94, Grant Avenue began its history.

In August of 1891, a pulpit committee recommended Reverend John Williams as pastor, and he answered their call until December of that year. At that time, J.J. Parten became pastor, and was with the church until April 1892. During his pastorate, a building committee was appointed, and a lot on the northeast corner of Grant and Poplar Streets was selected.

The Grant Street Baptist Church was built during the period of December 1893 to July 1894. Multiple pastors served the church during this time, and the church organized a First Missionary Society in 1897, with eight members.

By August of 1899, the church faced financial issues and little was recorded about the period from March of 1901 until January of 1902.

In January of 1902, it is recorded that a meeting was called and a resolution adopted to disband the church, and have the First Baptist Church take it over as a mission. The request was accepted and a superintendent, A.B. Lovan, was appointed for the Sunday School. He served for close to four years.

Once again, the church was able to organize. Reverend Zeb Thomas, who was employed by First Baptist Church as missionary pastor, called 70 members together and they subscribed to the Articles of Faith and Church Covenant. The new Grant Avenue Church was achieved on December 14, 1905. From this time forward, the church began to grow and show progress.

Trustees were elected in December of 1905, and in 1906, a Baptist Young Peoples Union (BYPU) and a Sunday School was organized. More recognition for the church came in 1907, when it was accepted into the Greene County Baptist Association. During this period, Reverend Thomas was with the church, but tendered his resignation in August of 1907. During that same month, Reverend T.G. Hendrix was called as pastor at a salary of $1,000.00 and the Women's Missionary Society was formed with eight members. During Reverend Hendrix's ministry, the West Side Mission was organized and the first building was erected on a lot on the corner of Nichols Street and Farmer Avenue. A Baptist Young People's Union was organized at the mission in 1911. A tent meeting was held on Eagle Avenue and 35 conversions were accepted. During this time, Reverend Hendrix's resignation was reluctantly accepted.

Records for the church were lost for the period of October 1913 through January of 1916, so little is known, with the exception that Reverend W.M. Braswell was extended a call and became pastor in October of 1913.

A nursery was set up in the church in 1917, with sixty babies enrolled in the Cradle Roll Department. A Royal Ambassador Chapter was organized, which is a mission discipleship program for boys in grades 1 through 6. The program helped the boys develop worldviews in relation to missions. They met on the first and fourth Sundays of the month. This was accomplished under the guidance of Reverend H.L. Aulick.

A roll call meeting was held in February of 1918, and the Ladies Aid Society served refreshments. The Ladies Aid Society also paid $100.00 per year of the pastor's salary.

Graded literature was used for the first time in the Sunday School in 1916, and during this time, many repairs and improvements were made in the church.

During the period from March 1919 to January 1920, the church voted to align with the Southern Baptist Convention. The membership roll was 323 with Sunday School at 250, supported by a staff of 15 teachers. The church budget was $3,000.00. The pastor's salary was $1,650.00, with a two-week, paid vacation. The pastor paid his own house rent. The value of the church property stood at $5,000.00.

The church had a magnificent growth period during 1920 through 1926. A new pastor, S.N. Mohler, accepted the church's call in February of 1920, and the church began to see great things for its future. Property was purchased on the corner of Grant Avenue and Scott Street. A house there was used as a parsonage, but with the idea of later building a new house of worship in the location. The parsonage was moved to 808 West Scott Street and the building project was begun in May of 1923, when a building committee was elected. The committee secured a plan that was submitted to the church and accepted on December 5, 1923.

A fundraising effort was started to move the plans forward with $18,000.00 being subscribed to complete the work. The first shovelful of dirt was turned to begin the project, as contributions were made and certificates were given to the contributors for the "bricks" that they purchased towards the erection of the new church. The cornerstone was laid in May of 1925. The contents included a Bible, Minutes of Greene County Association Meeting, a copy of the Articles of Faith, the Church Covenant and a list of the church membership. Issues of the newspapers published in the town of Springfield were also included in the cornerstone. When they disbanded, the Swedish Baptist Church gave their pulpit for the new church and it was still in use in 1991. The name of the church was changed from Grant Street Baptist Church to Grant Avenue Baptist Church when the city of Springfield changed the name of Grant Street to Grant Avenue.

The church petitioned the Circuit Court of Greene County for a Pro Forma Decree of Incorporation of the Grant Avenue Baptist Church. The petition was granted on March 9, 1925, and recorded by the clerk of the court.

A revival was held in February 1925, and 89 new members were added. During this time, the church voted that all funds go through a common treasurer and a financial secretary was named. The campaign of the Southern Baptist Convention received $5,000.00 towards its goal from the church.

During this time, the Sunday School was incredibly active and an attendance of 1,000 was recorded twice. Many worthwhile projects were started, including a Scout troop with a Scoutmaster named. Reverend Mohler tendered his resignation from the church in the latter part of 1925.

In June of 1926, worship services were held in the new building for the first time. The building was not complete, but the pews from the old building were brought in for seating and additional pews were purchased from the Central Christian Church. A new Pastor, T.H. Wiles, had come to the church in February and led the service. Things in the church were going well and active participation was visible in all of the Christian fellowship groups. Average attendance at the reorganized Sunday School was 350. The Missionary Society had seven circles and was supporting two Bible women in China. Also, the Baptist Young People's Union at the church continued to grow and won many honors at the state convention in 1932-1933.

A 24-member orchestra was formed in the church, and they performed at many of the church services and gave special concerts. In July of 1927, a Men's Brotherhood was organized and initially attended by 67 men.

Vacation Bible School was held in June of 1935, with 147 enrolled and 10 faculty members. The cost of the school for that summer was $45.85.

When the first anniversary for the new building was held in 1927, a large homecoming and dinner was served in the lower temple. In the afternoon, Brother T.E. Henderson delivered a speech on how the church was built. The anniversary celebration was held each year for the next ten years or so.

During the years of the 1920s and the 1930s, much growth was exhibited. About 775 members were received. The greatest growth was in development of worship, teaching, and training. Reverend Wiles's main interest during his time with the church was the children of the Junior Department of the Sunday School. He tried to lead each child to the Savior before that child left the department. Evangelistic services, held in the Junior Department at the Sunday School hour, saw many conversions. The church had many children join when Pastor Wiles was at the church. He resigned from the church in July of 1937.

Reverend C.A. Butler came to the church in February 1938, and remained until September of 1945. In 1938, a Mission Sunday School was started in a building rented on Chestnut Street. In April 1944, the old parsonage was sold and a new one purchased. Ten revivals were held during the time that Reverend Butler was at the church and 506 additions were made.

A mortgage held on the church building was paid off in January 1945. A mortgage burning celebration was held, and the church was dedicated in a special ceremony. In 1945, Reverend Butler left the church to accept the position of Superintendent of Missions in Los Angeles.

In September of 1950, the church installed a library. Much care and work was devoted to selecting and cataloguing books suitable for this purpose. Some needed repairs were completed at the parsonage, and the funds needed were included in the church budget. In February, the church purchased a house adjoining the church property on the west. It was redecorated and used as a nursery.

The church was still without a permanent pastor at the helm, and though calls were accepted, the tenures from the clergymen were short. Then in April of 1951, Glenn E. Bryant came to the church. He remained until 1957. Under his leadership, in and around 1952, the church began to realize the building was no longer able to meet the needs of its members. The pastor was given the authority to appoint a building committee and property south of the church was purchased and readied for Sunday School classrooms. Rooms under current use were outgrown and Vacation Bible School had outgrown the space used.

In June of 1953, to take care of anticipated expenses from the new buildings, the church raised over $50,000.00 to augment the building fund. This enabled building to begin earlier than anticipated and dedication services were held on October 3, 1954. The final cost of the new buildings, including the land, amounted to $192,227.00. As stated in the centennial book, this dollar amount does not and can never include the services and dedication of so many church members who worked and advised on the project.

On October 14, 1953, the church began broadcasting worship services on KTTS radio and a weekly 30-minute television program titled "Life at its Best." The television program was discontinued by June of 1957, but the radio broadcast continued until at least 1967.

A house and lot were purchased on West Scott Street in 1954, for $6,500.00 and the house was used as a Sunday School annex. Another house at the corner of Sunshine Street and Jefferson Avenue was purchased and was used to establish a branch church. The branch was opened and dedicated in April of 1956. Many families transferred to the new church. The financing was accomplished using $500.00 cash from the church funds, $10,000.00 borrowed from the State Mission Board, and a $12,000.00 mortgage was assumed. Visitation during Evangelism week in March of 1956, was tallied at 201 persons. Notable among the highlights of 1956, was the addition of 21 persons during a March revival.

In April of 1956, funeral services were held to honor Miss Florence Jones, who passed away after she had dedicated many years of service as a Missionary Nurse in China. Her work there spanned the years from 1907 to 1941. She was remembered for her remarkable accomplishment of dedication and service.

Good growth was noted in the church in 1956, as 177 additions were added at Grant Avenue and 38 were added at the Jefferson Avenue church. Grant Avenue Baptist was attracting many members from the surrounding neighborhoods. Enrollment for both locations for Sunday School was 1213. Vacation Bible School for the following year totaled 524 with an average attendance of 441.

The church budget for the next year, 1958, was set at $58,000.00 and approved. As the pulpit committee once again began searching for a new pastor, a church vote in September of 1957, changed the voting procedure for the acceptance of a new pastor. Now a pastor would not be called with less than 90% of the affirmative votes cast when previously only 51% was required. The new voting terms were used to accept Dr. J.P. Dane, who would began his post as of December 1, 1957.

A contract to install air conditioning in the sanctuary, at a cost of $10,347.00, was approved in April of 1958. $4,000.00 of that amount was paid from a fund set aside for that purpose. The balance was paid within 90 days to avoid interest. By the end of 1958, membership numbers had climbed at Grant Avenue to 1483, which does not include those who had transferred to Jefferson Street.

In the early part of 1959, at the death of Mrs. Lois Carter, the church accepted the responsibility for staffing the Cleveland Avenue Mission, a rescue mission that Mrs. Carter began to fulfill the spiritual and physical needs of the homeless in Springfield. The intent was to turn the mission over to the Greene County Association. In the interim a director, Reverend Joe Sands, was appointed. He was serving as pastor of the Cleveland Mission and appointed director in 1961. Reverend Sands and his wife remained as directors until August of

1967, when they accepted a similar position in Kansas City. Interim directors were named.

Additional property was purchased for parking at the church in 1960, and once again, the pulpit committee began a search for a new pastor to fill the position that would be vacated in the new year. Multiple times during the history of this church, pastors came and stayed for short periods. A new constitution was adopted in 1960, and was voted to supersede all other constitutions. It was hoped that the church would hold a spring revival in 1961, even though they were without a pastor, but the plans were later cancelled. The pulpit committee was very active and found a new pastor, Robert Taylor. He was to assume his duties in March of 1961, but declined to accept the church's offer, and again the pulpit committee began to search.

By June 11, 1961, Dr. Blake Westmorland would preach his first sermon at the church. He would stay with the church until June of 1973. In June, an Enlargement Campaign was started to contact 360 homes assigned to Grant Avenue after Robberson Avenue Baptist (later named Second Baptist) moved to a new location. Twenty-seven teams conducted the survey.

In June of 1962, the constitution of the church was amended to increase the number of deacons from fifteen to eighteen, and by the end of 1962, church membership stood at 1,492 with average Sunday School attendance at 463.

In June of 1963, Dr. Westmorland received formal expression of gratitude from Greene County Ministerial Alliance for his able defense of attacks on the Baptist denomination. In September of that year, a pastor's assistant was elected for visitation and education.

In August of 1964, the church was invited to participate in the International Pastor Exchange Program. Dr. Westmorland and his wife went to Falkirk, Scotland, to represent Grant Avenue, and Reverend John Lyons, from the Falkirk Church, occupied the pulpit at Grant Avenue as his part in the exchange. In 1965, Grant Avenue completed modernizing the balcony in their church's building. In September, the Cleveland Avenue Mission, sponsored by Grant Avenue, was renamed Grand Oak Center and rededicated.

The parsonage of the church was badly in need of repairs, and a committee recommended the house be sold. The pastors of the church would then obtain their own housing, with a monthly allowance to compensate them for the rent. The parsonage was sold for $11,000.00 in 1967, ending the church's responsibility of repairs and maintenance.

During May of 1968, Dr. Westmorland was awarded a singular honor when he was invited to attend a meeting at the Union Theological Seminary in New York, as this invitation is extended to only twenty representatives of major denominations. In July of that year, the mortgage against church property was paid in full leaving the church indebtedness of other expenses at $56,295.00. The church purchased a 12-passenger van in September to be used as transportation for church affairs as needed, and it was immediately put into service. By the end of the year, church indebtedness had slightly declined, and balance of available funds was $12,648.00.

Dr. Westmorland, who spent his early ministerial life in an economically-depressed area of a Kentucky coalmining community, expressed concern that the church may be neglecting the same in Springfield. In 1970, a new staff position, "Director of Community Services" was added to reach out in social services in the city. The first issue of a newsletter, "Ave-a-News," was issued to keep members abreast of matters of interest in the church. In July, the WMU and the Brotherhood organizations were combined to eliminate duplication of activities. The church had one revival in the year 1970, and the budget for the upcoming year was set at $88,400.00.

A larger form of transportation was needed and the church purchased a 42-passenger bus. It was painted white, with the name of the church painted in blue on the sides. In January 1971, the church purchased two houses immediately adjacent to the church on the south for the sum of $12,500.00. In July, Dr. Westmorland began a series of five-minute talks on KWFC Radio, at a cost of $20.00 per week. The budget for the church continued to grow with the next year's (1972) at $91,000.00. A long range planning committee was formed to determine opportunities for service, and needs for the future. They were asked to take time to deliberate carefully before making their recommendations. Their first recommendation came in September of 1972. They recommended that the sanctuary be completely refurbished. In December, the church voted to pave and fence a lot west of the alley to add 15 more parking spaces. The cost would be $3,449.00. The average attendance at Sunday School for the year was 330.

Dr. Westmorland, who had served the church since June of 1961, tendered his resignation and left the church in July of 1973. A pulpit committee was appointed to begin the search for his replacement. The outgoing pastor was honored with a going-away program, which filled the pews of the church. Dr. Westmorland was well thought of for his writings, which appeared weekly in the church newsletter, "The Grant Ave-a-News." He had written many essays, which he called "From a Worm's Eye View," and he was pleased that all 156 of his essays had been published in book form as a going away surprise. Church members had accomplished the publication of the book through donations towards the purchase of the book. He autographed each book, and the event was published in the *Springfield News Leader*. Dr. Westmorland's tenure was the longest of any pastor at the church. He served for thirteen years.

Once Dr. Westmorland left the church, there was an interim time without a pastor that lasted until March of 1974. Work and progress at the church continued as the search for a new pastor was underway. In September of 1973, the church voted to refurbish the sanctuary at a cost of approximately $40,000.00, with a radical change in the décor from French Provincial to Modern Danish. A sale of the French Provincial decorator items removed from the church was held for members. The year 1973 closed with a slight loss of membership. Sunday School attendance averaged of 286. The value of church property was $368,000.00.

By February of 1974, the refurbishing of the sanctuary was completed, and James A. Woods, Jr. accepted the pastorate. Pastor Woods held spring revivals, and Vacation Bible School was attended by 362 youth. A special service was held to commemorate the 83rd anniversary of the church's first organization on July 26, 1891. The year closed with a slight increase in membership and the largest budget to date, $104,500.00.

Janice Sartin was employed as a nursery-kindergarten director, effective in June of 1977. She is a seminary graduate, and she remains an important part of the youth effort at the church to this day. In addition, in 1977, a plan to begin a ministry to "exceptional young people" was reported and a couple from Southwest Baptist College, with experience in the field, was contacted to begin the program. The church year ended uneventfully with additions to membership, which was now at 884, with Sunday School attendance at 249.

A married couple, John and Christina Aderinto from Africa, were given sponsorship by the church for admission to Southwestern Baptist Seminary. They hoped to complete their studies and return to Africa, where they reported much work needed to be done. They made a presentation to the church dressed in their native costumes. They expressed their concern over the needs in their country and the difficulties they would endure to prepare themselves for their mission.

The deacons of the church began a "family ministry" in the late 1970s. Members of the church would be assigned to help deal with the more personal issues. New members would be given individualized attention to help welcome them into the church. A special fund raising "gospel sing" was held to support the efforts of medical workers in Haiti, where it was reported the need was great.

In January of 1979, value of church property was reported at over a million dollars for insurance purposes. Grand Oak Baptist Mission celebrated its 25th anniversary. The mission efforts had been successful, and Grant Avenue Baptist would continue as a sponsor. The church continued to be without a permanent pastor and several interim pastors had served. A vote to continue support for the Aderinto family from Africa was approved. They were attending Southwestern Baptist Seminary, and would continue there for two more years, as John Aderinto sought his advanced degree before the family returned home to begin their work.

Dr. George T. Miller began his service to the church as of August 1979. His tenure with the church would continue until June of 1985. By the end of 1979, church membership stood at 896 and Sunday School averaged 225. A new group for seniors in the church was begun called B.A.L.L. (Be active live longer.) The church mourned the loss of several long-term members including George West, who served as a deacon for forty years.

Grant Avenue was honored to be ranked sixth out of 64 participants, to exceed Sunday School goals by churches participating in the Baptist Association in 1980. Also in 1980, the 89th anniversary of the church was observed with a homecoming and carry-in dinner. In November, approval was received to set up a fund to purchase a van to carry approximately 15 people. Sunday services at Grand Oak Mission were discontinued, and those wishing to attend services would be bused to Grant Avenue. The 15-passenger van was acquired in July of 1981, with funds from the estates of several long-term members, as well as other memorial funds.

In 1982, Grant Avenue received the "Eagle Award," which represents outstanding efforts of the Sunday School program. Three hundred churches in the Southern Baptist Convention participate in the program, and only 36 churches in the SBC had received the award in the past years.

Space was selected in a Lee Street store building for Fellowship Mission, with the first service to be April 4 of 1982. A survey was conducted by 15 members to locate prospects for the new mission. Grant Avenue would contribute $75.00 per week to help defray expenses at the mission.

A special program, on a Sunday morning in September, was held to dedicate a new grand piano to the memory of Deacon Edwin C. Johnson, which had been bought with funds donated by his family. Mr. Johnson had a long-time wish to provide the instrument for the church. Total membership at the end of 1982, stood at 963. Throughout the year, the church made special offerings of over $6,700.00 to missions — home, state and foreign. Dr. Miller was committed to mission offerings, and urged liberal giving for foreign missions.

In 1983, Grant Avenue Baptist was invited to participate in the Springfield Area Council of Churches' efforts to compile a 100-year history of churches in Greene County. The years covered were 1833 through 1933. A committee was drawn up to write Grant Avenue's part in the history, and copies were provided to the congregation. The book was entitled *The History of the Churches in Greene County, Mo.* In November, an interim pastor was called at the Fellowship Mission.

Dr. Miller celebrated his 25th year in the ministry in 1984, and the church helped him rejoice with a carry-in dinner. Dr. Miller earned his doctorate through correspondence courses, which was considered an exemplary accomplishment. The long-range planning committee sadly reports that average Sunday School attendance continued to decline. It currently stood at 266 but was at 412 twenty years prior. Dr. Miller presented his plans to conduct backyard Bible studies in August, for the youth in Grant Beach Park area.

In April of 1985, deacons from the church recommended that Grant Avenue participate in a citywide campaign, "Good News Revival," and the church donated $500.00 to help defray expenses.

In the spring, Dr. Miller called an all-church meeting to consider the future of Grant Avenue. The decisions about the church's future included remaining in the same location after assessing the community needs. Any option considered was to dispose of the current property and relocate to the southern part of the city, where the heaviest growth was occurring. In addition, it was recommended that the present property be kept and maintained as a type of mission center. The discussions that followed generated a great deal of interest, and the meetings were very well attended. At the conclusion of the assessment, after a considerable amount of time had been spent, a vote was taken and the majority voted in favor of keeping the church in the current location.

In June of 1985, shortly after the Southern Baptist Convention in St. Louis, Dr. Miller tendered his resignation from the church. An associate pastor was asked to act as interim pastor, as a pulpit committee was appointed and a pastor sought.

In July of 1985, the city of Springfield established new safety codes for day care centers, requiring Grant Avenue to upgrade in order to comply and continue their program. A vote was taken to continue the day care, and an estimate of $30,000.00 would be necessary to bring the church into compliance with the new codes. An increase in fees would be required to defray part of the expense, and the congregation was asked for goodwill offerings to help with the expense. By November, over $21,000.00 was received for the project.

The Fellowship Mission called a new pastor, in November, to replace a pastor who resigned. No revivals were held in 1985, and total receipts for the church topped $213,000.00, with the value of property just slightly over a million dollars.

The plans to bus members from Grand Oak Mission to Grant Avenue for services had not gone as hoped. It was felt that Grant Avenue should no longer sponsor Grand Oak, but it should come under the

Grant Avenue Baptist Church, 1984

sponsorship of all the churches in the association, which was accepted and put into effect. Many from Grant Avenue still devoted their energies to the mission.

After considering 54 resumes, in March of 1986, the pulpit committee offered leadership of the church to Michael Lockhart. The church was once again with a pastor after a vacancy of nine months. Pastor Lockhart's first sermon was delivered on April 13th.

Shortly after Pastor Lockhart's arrival, he, along with the deacons, trustees, and other church members, began addressing concerns over the condition of the church property. Much time and effort were devoted to this project. Estimates for the needed work were sought, and the membership was asked for volunteers for cleaning and refurbishing. The effort was done on a continuing basis, with the concerns of the greatest problems dealt with first.

By July of 1988, Pastor Lockhart had left the church and the church would soon be turning to its centennial, which loomed in 1991. Once again, a pulpit search committee was appointed. An interim pastor, and a church administrator to oversee the church business, were approved to serve while a permanent pastor was called. This interim period lasted until July of 1989, when Reverend Gary "Rick" Hedger was asked to accept the call of the pulpit committee.

In January of 1990, Reverend Hedger led a Lay Evangelism Conference and invited his brother-in-law, Reverend Rick Ferguson, pastor of a church in DeSoto, Missouri, to lead a one day, intense "Soul Winning Workshop." Participating members then went out into the community, with encouraging results, and several new members were added to the church.

In May of 1990, a centennial planning committee was appointed and approved, and the church began to looking forward to the celebration of its 100th birthday. Also in May, a spring revival was held, with guest from a Baptist church in Fort Worth, Texas, sharing the pulpit.

The members and pastor of Freedom Baptist Church in Springfield were invited to Grant Avenue, as the church was struggling with financial problems. Grant Avenue offered their help, including free childcare for the pastor's wife so she could seek employment.

A group of members from Grant Avenue traveled to Polytechnic Baptist Church, in July of 1990, to help with much needed carpentry work at a center where the children of the church met. The church,

Grant Avenue Baptist Church

which was in Fort Worth, Texas, was located in the inner city and its needs were challenging. It was a moving and rewarding experience, especially for the youth of the church who joined the effort.

A faulty light fixture in a storage room of the day care center caused considerable smoke damage when fire broke out at the church on July 20, 1990. It was necessary to cancel day care service for several days. On Sunday, July 23, over 200 members met under a rented tent for services due to the extensive smoke damage caused by the fire. It was heartwarming to see the amount of care, concern and help offered by other churches in the area. The incident drew the members closer together when the realization came that the fire could have caused the loss of their church building. Clean up efforts continued through the following weeks and months.

A special business meeting, following worship service on August 19, was called to discuss purchasing property just south of the church. The asking price was over $40,000.00, and the purchase was rejected, as the cost was too high. Ultimately, the price for the property was reduced and the land is used for additional parking.

On December 30, 1990, winter weather hit the Ozarks, with ice bringing hazardous conditions. A thick coat of ice blanketed the town of Springfield. Many churches cancelled services, but Grant Avenue held its service as usual. Only 35 attended the services with 28 at Sunday School. The evening services were cancelled.

By year's end, a total of $111,254.00 had been spent to repair and clean damage caused by the fire at the church in July. Insurance reimbursed the church for all but a small amount due to deductibles and depreciation. The church finished the year with a membership of 892, with a loss of members standing at 44.

Plans for the centennial committee kick off were cancelled due to the weather in December of 1990, and the next meeting was scheduled for February, 1991. The ice storm that struck in December still held the city in its grip, and attendance at church was well below normal.

When the committee met, a decision to wear old fashioned dress during the three days of the celebration was thought to add to the atmosphere. Plans for the celebration included a banquet, with the director of the Missouri Baptist Association as guest speaker. An ice cream social would be held with special mention of the fact that the day care was celebrating its 50th anniversary. Throughout the celebration, multiple activities had been planned, with music an integral part of the festivities. A time capsule was buried containing various memorabilia from the church's 100-year history including current editions of newspapers with the news of the day, a copy of the Centennial Church Bulletin, and a copy of the Church Pictorial Directory. A banner, which had hung in the sanctuary announcing the centennial motto, "Onward and Upward," was also placed in the capsule, and an engraved memorial plaque covers the capsule. The spirit of the church for the future, its dreams and plans, were now placed in the capable hands of the disciples.

The last reported membership of 892, was from 1990, with the Sunday School attendance at 199. Membership during the 1960s stood close to 1,500, making Grant Avenue Baptist one of the largest in the city. In the year 2016, the church celebrated another anniversary, their 125th. According to an article in the *Springfield News Leader* Newspaper on July 16, 2016, only about 60 people worship at the church on

Grant Avenue Baptist Church, 2017

Sunday mornings, but the church has made an indelible mark on the city and the people who live here. Thousands have walked through its doors and worshiped at its altar. The Reverend Roy Roach, who has served the church for the past year or more, said the church's plan is to focus on the area and neighborhoods around Grant Beach to determine the ministries that are needed. The church will never be the dynamic institution it once was, but the church will thrive in its current environment. Like so many churches in the north of Springfield, attendance has dropped as the growth of the city has rapidly moved to the south. The church has a warm, powerful legacy having founded two other churches in Springfield and supported the Grand Oak Mission. The church, for now, is still clinging to the motto that served them for one hundred years, "Onward and Upward."

Current Information

1003 North Grant Avenue
(417) 869-0548
www.facebook.com/grantavebaptist

Resources Used

Bartee, Wayne C., *Greene County Baptist Churches in Ministry, 1838-1984*

Fairbanks and Tuck, *Past and Present Greene County, Missouri,* 1915

Moser, Arthur Paul, *Churches in Greene County, MO*, 1983

Special Centennial Edition – Grant Avenue Baptist Church – July 26, 1891 to July 26, 1991- prepared by multiple church members from church records, individual accounts and historical data available from the church.

The Springfield New Leader – July 16, 2016

www.facebook.com/grantavebaptist

Boulevard Baptist Church, 1891
Pythian (Avenue) Baptist Church, 1912
Just for Jesus Church, 2016

In January 1891, a Sunday School was started in the Boulevard Hotel. In the summer, they met under a grove of trees at the foot of Prospect Street Hill. A tent revival was held, and, in August of that year, the group organized into the Boulevard Baptist Church. First Baptist Church donated a lot on the corner of North Rogers and George (now Pythian) Streets. Mr. E.M. Shepherd was instrumental in getting local businessmen to donate $800 toward the construction of a new building on the lot. Initially, the building was also used as a Knights of Pythian meeting place. When George Street was changed to Pythian Avenue, the church became known as the Pythian Avenue Baptist Church.

Hard times fell on the group after 1900, and First Baptist Church took on the work as a mission. Funds were given, and new members joined the group as they continued their work. By 1912, the group was able to become self supporting and go back to church status. Rev. Lynn Swadley, Sr., served two pastorates and was an effective leader, helping the church to eliminate their debt and expand their facilities. He was able to set the church on a stable course, including a church budget and organizational growth.

In the last few years, church membership had declined and the future existence seemed bleak. Another group of believers was growing

Pythian Avenue Baptist Church, 1984

Just for Jesus Church, 2017

and needing a larger meeting facility. The two groups eventually met and discussed the possibility of a merger. The merger was agreed to in 2016, with the new name Just for Jesus Church.

Current Information

1001 North Rogers Avenue
(417) 862-5386
www.facebook.com/Pythian-Ave-Baptist-Church-121447181/about

Resources Used

Bartee, Wayne C., *Greene County Baptist in Ministry, 1838-1984*
Moser, Arthur Paul, *Churches in Greene County, MO*, 1983
www.facebook.com/Pythian-Ave-Baptist-Church-121447181/about

St. Joseph's Catholic Church, 1892

In 1892, there were already two Catholic churches in Springfield: Immaculate Conception and Sacred Heart. With many German immigrants settling in Springfield, the German Catholics were not comfortable in the existing churches. Many could not speak English or understand Latin. They wanted their own Catholic church. Many members of the existing churches were not inclined to support the Germans' desires. In 1892, a parish church was appointed for the German immigrants, comprised of about thirty families. Since the Germans were largely a poor group, it seemed unlikely that their hopes would be fulfilled.

However, a wealthy Springfield businessman came to the rescue. A record by Father Mauris Eckstein, published in 1907, reported:

> *Mr. Chas. Heer, a devout Catholic, noticing for years how the German Catholics were drifting away from God and their religion, nourished the earnest desire to see a Catholic church erected for the German speaking Catholics. At this critical hour, therefore, he proposed on his own account, and with the consent of his wife and devoted children, a house and lot, valued at $10,000, for the aforesaid purpose. The most generous offer soon encouraged others. And many of the good hearted people of Springfield, Catholics and non-Catholics, gave a helping hand in different ways and according to their means. In addition to Mr. Heer's donation, a subscription of $3,000 was made up for the erection of the building necessary for church and college.*

The building, at 807 North Jefferson Avenue, was dedicated on February 5, 1893. This modest chapel adequately served the congregation.

St. Joseph's Catholic Church under construction, 1905-06

On April 3, 1898, Charles H. Heer, Sr. died. In his will he bequeathed $15,000 to the church and

St. Joseph's Catholic Church after completion in 1906

$1,000 to the school. By 1904, the congregation grew to include 75 families and there was a need for larger facilities. There were tensions with the location, at that time, being so close to Immaculate Conception.

Three lots were purchased at the corner of Campbell Avenue and Scott Street. Ground was broken for a new concrete church building in the fall of 1904. Dedicaion services for the debt-free church were held November 29, 1906. Three additional lots on Scott Street were purchased in April, 1907.

The rectory was completed in 1908. In 1925, major additions were made to the sanctuary with a Wicks Direct Electric Pipe Organ and a set of Deagan tower chimes. Very little history of the church is found in the early Depression years. During these years the church continued to support an active school. In 1934, the congregation had grown to 156 families, with 97 students enrolled in the school. In 1939, a complete new lighting system was installed. Major renovations were also made inside and outside of the church in preparation for the Golden Anniversary in 1942.

Aerial photo of St. Joseph's Catholic Church, ca. 1942

A new brick school was dedicated in 1950, and a second floor added to it in 1955. Continued building and site improvements were made in the late 1950s and early 1960s. The Vatican Council II reforms in the mid-1960s created changes in the sanctuary, with the altar facing the people and other renovations. At the 75th anniversary celebration on November 29, 1981, the Heritage Room (historical records) was dedicated.

St. Joseph's Catholic Church, 2017

In 1976, the church was officially added to the National Historic Registry. Additional staff was hired in the late 1970s and 1980s to provide for increased social, educational and ministry activities. Another round of building improvements was made in the 1990s anticipating the centennial celebration in 1992.

In 1999, Father Denis Dougherty, OSB, began his service as pastor. He continues in that capacity to this day. He graciously provided materials and encouragement for this book. The church has a thriving food assistance program, as well as many other community ministries.

Current Information

1115 North Campbell Avenue
(417) 865-1112
www.stjosephsmo.org

Resources Used

Centennial, St. Joseph's Church, 1906-2006. Printed and bound by Print Group Inc., Ozark, Missouri. Celebrated November 26, 2006

http://the library.org/lochist/postcards/st_josephs.cfm

Pastva, Loretta, *The Catholic Church in Southern Missouri, 1956-2006*

St. Joseph's Parish, Springfield, Missouri, 1892-1992 Centennial

The Centennial of St. Joseph's Church, 1892-1992. Theresa A. Bade, Editor, April, 1992

www.stjosephsmo.org

Ray Chapel Baptist Church, 1895 Hamlin Memorial Baptist Church, 1908

On March 8, 1892, the Robberson Avenue Baptist Church (currently Second Baptist Church) organized a mission in the northwestern part of the city. An active member of the founding church, William Ray, was instrumental in organizing the mission, securing a building site and serving as treasurer of the new mission. On March 1, 1893, $350 was borrowed at 8% interest, repayable at $100 a year, to purchase the mission building at the corner of Grant Avenue and Kearney Street. The church was organized in June 1895, and named in honor of William Ray, as Ray Chapel Baptist Church. There were seven charter members. The first pastor was A.B. Elsey. Within a year, the membership had grown to twenty-seven.

In November 1907, Rev. J.R. Hamlin became pastor. His son, O.T. Hamlin, was an attorney. He suggested that the church move toward center city for convenience and security. He donated a lot at the corner of High and Main Streets, and a new structure was built in 1908. The church was renamed, in honor of their pastor and his wife, as the Hamlin Memorial Baptist Church.

The church began to grow rapidly, and by 1918, it reached over 500 members. Outgrowing its smaller structure, a new basement building and site was completed in 1922, at the present location of Missouri and Atlantic. A new building was completed in 1925, that seated 600 and had ten rooms. The cost was $45,000.

In 1929, Reverend Haskel T. Abbott began a lengthy pastorate over nearly twenty-five years. At that time, the church membership was

Hamlin Memorial Baptist Church

Hamlin Memorial Baptist Church, 2016

807. In spite of the Depression era struggles, the church continued to grow in number and facilities. Nearby houses were purchased for use as Sunday School classrooms. Upon Reverend Abbott's retirement, the membership had grown to 1,594 members. In the last half of the 1950s, a new education building was added, with ten departmental rooms, twenty-six additional classrooms, five nurseries, a library, an office suite and a recreation room.

In the 1960s, the sanctuary was extensively remodeled. In the 1970s, nearby properties were purchased for additonal parking space. Hamlin was one of the earliest churches to begin a bus ministry to reach out to the community. A Christian Life Center was decicated on April 24, 1988. Costs exceeded over one million dollars.

During its history, the church was also able to sponsor several church starts in north Springfield: Northwest (Sunset Chapel), 1919; Bethlehem Chapel, 1941 (later dissolved); and Fremont Baptist Church, 1963.

In 2015, the church explored a move from a declining neighborhood. They decided on land just north of the interstate on Highway 13. Construction was started and hoped to be completed in 2017. In October of 2016, the church discussed what to do with their present building facilities, valued at over one million dollars. It was agreed to donate the property for community activities and continued ministry. In April 2017, the church moved to the new location on Highway 13.

Hamlin Memorial Baptist Church at its new location on Highway 13, 2017

Current Information

829 West Atlantic Street
(417) 869-4694
www.hamlinbaptist.com/

Resources Used

Bartee, Wayne C., *Greene County Baptist in Ministry, 1838-1984*
Moser, Arthur Paul, *Churches in Greene County*, 1983
Printed materials provided by the church office
www.hamlinbaptist.com/

Reorganized Latter Day Saints Church, 1896 Community of Christ, Central Congregation, 2001

Since its founding, the Reorganized Latter Day Saints have always fought being labeled as "Mormon," however, they do trace their origins back to Joseph Smith. Upon Joseph Smith's death in Carthage, Illinois, in 1844, division arose among the large group of followers left in Nauvoo, Illinois. The great majority followed the leadership of Brigham Young, and made the long trek to what was to become Salt Lake City, Utah. A sizeable minority, left behind in Nauvoo, followed the direct descendants of Joseph Smith to the previously designated center place of Zion - Independence, Missouri. There they established their world headquarters.

Although they accept the Book of Mormon and some of Joseph Smith's early revelation as scripture in the Doctrine and Covenants, they refuse to accept later parts of the Book of Commandments and the Pearl of Great Price as valid scripture. They have actively sent church missionaries into all corners of the country and the world. They have grown and prospered as a religious body. Presidents of the body have traditionally been descendants of Joseph Smith. However, in the 1980s and 1990s, President Wallace B. Smith made numerous significant reforms in the church's operations. Among these were the ordination of women into the preisthood, opening Communion to all Christians, and building bridges with other religious groups.

In 1996, President Wallace Smith named W. Grant McMurray as his presidential successor, the first time without a direct descendant of Joseph Smith being head of the church. Other reforms were made, with the major one happening in 2001. A new name was chosen, Community of Christ. The new name reflected the mission of the church, while creating distance from the erroneous identity with the Mormons.

After McMurray's retirement in 2005, Stephen M. Veazey was ordained as the eighth prophet-president of the church. He has worked toward greater diversity in the church and expansion in the world.

Central Community of Christ, 2017

Current Information

2722 North National Avenue
(417) 865-6195
www.centralcofchrist.org

Resources Used

Correspondence with Rachel Killebrew, Community of Christ Archivist, October, 2016

Fairbanks and Tuck, *Past and Present Greene County, Missouri*, 1915

Saints' Herald Archives

www.cofchrist.org/history

www.latterdaytruth.org

Seventh Day Adventist, 1899

We had hoped to include more information about this church. Yet, after repeated contact attempts, the church has not responded to our requests for information on their organizational history. We have found some limited information from secondary sources that we have included.

Seventh Day Adventists claim acknowledgement as a Protestant denomination. Although some of their stated doctrinal beliefs may coincide with traditional Protestant theology, some of their practices and their disassociation with nationalistic and societal responsibilities have led to criticism. They offer many humanitarian services to the community.

The Adventists trace their origin back to the Millerites of New England in the 1840s. They came to a strong belief that Jesus would return to earth on October 22, 1844. When Jesus did not return on that day, many left the faith and returned to former churches. Others continued in the faith, realizing errors in Miller's computations. Those remaining began to solidify their other beliefs and practices. The idea of a Sabbath-keeping doctrine was influenced by Joseph Bates in the late 1840s. It wasn't until May 21, 1863, that the group officially organized in Battle Creek, Michigan. The denominational headquarters made several moves, finally settling in Silver Springs, Maryland.

The church groups began to increase in evangelistic fervor as they reached westward in the United States. They also began ministries in Switzerland, Russia, Ghana, South Africa and Japan. The movement in the United States led to organizational and administrative divisions. Their work in Missouri is part of the Mid-America Union Conference.

Seventh Day Adventist Springfield, 2017

It is not known exactly when the work came to Springfield, but the group was mentioned in a 1915 listing of churches. It was listed as having begun in 1899. Today there are two, primary Seventh Day Adventist churches in Springfield. They also operate a school.

Current Information

702 South Belview Avenue
(417) 865-5226
www.springfieldsda.org/

Resources Used

nadadventist.org
www.springfieldsda.org/

First Church of Christ, Scientist, 1899

Several sources chronicle the beginnings of the First Church of Christ, Scientist in Springfield, Missouri, as July of 1897, with the true organization of the church occurring in December of 1899, when their charter was granted. However, the followers of Mary Baker Eddy in Springfield, in accounts of their own history, note a date as early as 1893, when meetings were held in private homes in north and south Springfield. This 1893 date is just six years shy of the date when the first Christian Science Church was built in the United States at Oconto, Wisconsin.

In 1898, those who were meeting north of Springfield rented a room in an academic building on the campus of Drury University, which they used through November of that year. In December of 1899, Louise Egan and her daughter, Ester L. Egan, applied for a charter for a Church of Christ, Scientist from the state of Missouri. They are credited with the first published mention of the Christian Science Church in Springfield, when their practitioner cards were published in the Christian Science Journal of 1897-1898. (A practitioner is recognized as an individual who has completed extensive training in the art of healing and health based on the teaching of the Bible and the work and books written by Mary Baker Eddy. Once a practitioner is accredited, they devote their ministry to prayerful healing and may promote their practice in the pages of The Christian Science Monitor, which is published monthly in 12 languages and online.)

Regular meetings of members were held in the home of Mrs. Emma Thompson on Mount Vernon Street, when she moved to Springfield in 1893, until services and a Reading Room were opened in the Baldwin Theatre building on St. Louis Street. The first lecture on Christian Science in Springfield was delivered by Judge William G. Ewing of Chicago at the Baldwin Theatre on March 23, 1903. This theatre, and several other buildings, were destroyed by fire in January of 1909.

In June of 1903, Ester Egan, daughter of the late Louise Egan, asked the church to accept the state charter applied for in 1899, which had never been used. The church was then recognized by the state of Missouri, and published in the Christian Science publication.

When the Baldwin Theatre was no longer available for services, private homes were used for gatherings until June of 1903, when a building formerly used by Congregationalists at West Walnut and Market Streets

The first building used by First Church of Christ, Scientist

was rented. There, Sunday services, Sunday School and Wednesday meetings were conducted and a Reading Room was established.

In 1908, the church moved to the new Masonic Temple building on Walnut Street where they held services until 1911. It was then the church board began to consider taking action to find a permanent home for the church in their own building. After many months of consideration, and evaluating various locations in Springfield, a parcel of land on East Central Street across from the public library was purchased in February, 1915. Generous provisions in the will of Mary Baker Eddy, in her desire to help finance branch churches, were used to help with the purchase of the lot for the sum of $1,502.50. The Reading Room was moved to the Woodruff building in a space rented for $25.00 per month.

The church members pledged to pay part of the $10,000.00 needed to construct the building, and a contract with a builder was signed in July of 1915. When complete, the church cost $13,700.84. Of that amount, $5,513.04 had come from the Trustees of the Mary Baker Eddy will and the church repaid the amount to the mother church in July 1967.

The desire to celebrate the first service in their new church building in December of 1915, did not occur due to delays in finishing the building. The first service was celebrated in January of 1916. At the time of the first services, average attendance was 140. The official dedication was held in June of 1916. This building now houses part of the Greene County Health Department.

The church building was praised by architects as one of the most artistic in the state. It was designed by architect, church member, and First Reader Arch N. Torbitt.

At the time of construction, the front of the building displayed three arched windows containing stained glass panels in an Italian Renaissance pattern, which at the time were the most expensive of any church in Springfield. The center panel displayed the emblem of the church first used by Mary Baker Eddy in 1875 or 1876, the Cross and Crown. In the latter part of 1980, this stained glass panel was removed and sold to the Sixth Church of Christ, Scientist in Chicago, Illinois.

Since the church was built, it has gone through multiple renovations and improvements; some of them major, such as replacing the heating and installing a cooling system. In the beginning, a piano was used to provide music for the new church, until April of 1919, when an organ was purchased for the sum of $4,365.00.

The church has been involved in many events in the community including taking an active part during World War II. They contributed to the war effort, from sewing for war relief to furnishing wartime ministers at Fort Leonard Wood and the local USO.

The building at East Central Street successfully fulfilled the needs of the church for many years. Renovations had been made, but more costly updates needed to be satisfied. The main problem for the church was parking. There was no resolution for the parking problem and a search for a site to build a new church was begun around June of 1990. No satisfactory locations were found, but the city of Springfield had expressed an interest in the East Central Street building and now offered to help with finding a new location for the church. It was through their intervention that property was located on South Eastgate Avenue. A vote was held in January of 1991 on the purchase of the property, and the transaction was closed on May 23, 1991, with payment made in cash. The congregation began to plan and save for their new home. Ground was broken in December of 1992, and the architecture firm of Spencer Architects of Springfield was hired for the design. Since July 4, 1993, an attractive contemporary building with ample parking at 960 South Eastgate Avenue is home for the First Church of Christ, Scientist of Springfield, Missouri.

A new organ was purchased and donated by a member of the congregation, while the old organ was sold to a private party.

Churches of Christ, Scientist provide Reading Rooms, or libraries, to allow for a quiet atmosphere for the public to study and learn about the Church of Christ, Scientist or to read, study and pray. These rooms provide "a harbor of rest" from everyday life. The concepts for the room were established in 1899, with a bylaw in the manual of the mother church. They are open to the public. The First Church of Christ, Scientist Reading Room is currently located at 1950 South Glenstone Avenue. Prior to this location, it has been located in the Holland Building on the square, then the McDaniel Building on St. Louis Street, where it remained until 1954. A new location was established at 324 East Walnut Street, and then moved to 1675 East Seminole Street.

First Church of Christ, Scientist, 2017

Christian Science churches are found around the world and all are based on the Bible and the writings and teachings of Mary Baker Eddy. The church was founded in 1879 in Boston, Massachusetts, which is recognized as the mother church. The Boston church publishes bylaws to be used as a guide for other churches around the world, but each church authors its own bylaws and is independent from churches of the same name, although considered a branch of the mother church in Boston, Massachusetts.

The church has a board that governs and oversees decisions for the church. The board members serve a term of three years. There is no clergy in the church, and two Readers conduct services. The vast majority of the service is the reading of a weekly Bible lesson supplied by the Mother Church in Boston. Readers serve for a three-year period and are elected by the congregation. They are not authorized to officiate at weddings and the faith has no specific funeral requirements.

Current Information

960 South Eastgate Avenue
(417) 889-9604
www.facebook.com.First-Church-of-Christ

Resources Used

Fairbanks and Tuck, *Past and Present of Greene County, Missouri*, 1915

History of First Church of Christ, Scientist Springfield, Missouri 1893-1979 – from the historical records of the board of the church.

Springfield Greene County Library –Historical Postcards of Springfield, Missouri.

Wikipedia.org Church_ of_ Christ,_ Scientist

Chapter Six

1900s

Historical Notes (local, state and national)

The first decade of the 1900s saw Springfield continue its dramatic growth. The population increased from 23,000 to 35,200. Cows were still being herded through the streets as late as 1903. A public library opened in 1905, and the State Normal School (S.M.S.U. and now M.S.U.) opened in 1906 with 543 students. The first automobiles began to appear on the city streets.

Several influential residents began to expand the services in Springfield. On Thanksgiving Day, 1906, Ellen Burge donated her frame duplex on Jefferson Avenue to be used as a Methodist hospital. Originally called Burge Deaconess Hospital, it later was expanded and was renamed Lester E. Cox Hospital, after a successful expansion campaign. Another significant benefactor was John T. Woodruff. In 1907, he built the Sansone Hotel (now The Sterling) and then in 1911, the Woodruff Building (now Sky Eleven). He was also instrumental in securing the site for the new Springfield Normal School (now Missouri State University). He had great influence in construction of the Ozarks' major power and recreation sites.

Prejudice and lawlessness were still very present in the town. One of the saddest examples occurred in April 1906, when a mob of 5,000 witnessed the lynching of three blacks on the electric tower on the Public Square. The three were later found innocent of the charges of sexual assault and no one was ever declared guilty of the horrendous crime.

Churches Established No Longer Operating

Vesta Avenue Methodist Episcopal Church, 1902

The group was associated with Grace Methodist Church and later with Mount Carmel Methodist Church. They met in a wooden structure at the corner of Grant and Chestnut Streets.

Scene of a lynching of three men thought to be guilty of sexual assault, Easter Sunday, April 1906. The three were found innocent following their deaths.

Church of God Seventh Day, 1904

Metropolitan Colored Baptist Church, 1905

Originally, they met in a house of worship at the north end of Mount Vernon Avenue. Later, they moved to a new concrete building at the northwest corner of Vernon and High Streets.

Pilgrim Congregational Church, 1908

Churches Currently Operating

Woodland Heights Presbyterian Church, 1907

Central Assembly of God Church, 1907

St. Agnes Catholic Parish, 1908

Reunion Presbyterian Church, 1908 Woodland Heights Presbyterian Church, 1912

Woodland Heights Presbyterian Church

This church acknowledges its beginnings as May 31, 1908, when it was known as Reunion Presbyterian Church. The name was chosen as an acknowledgment of the joining of the Cumberland Presbyterian Church with the larger Presbyterian Church (USA) in May of 1906. Three Presbyterian ministers in Springfield, Missouri, could see a need for a church in the northwest part of the city. These churches supported the organization: First Cumberland Presbyterian, Calvary Presbyterian, and Second Presbyterian. It began with thirty-two charter members. A Sunday School preceded the church and dates were not given for its start, but perhaps a reference to a date of 1907 may have been for the Sunday School mission project.

In 1912, the church had grown and the number of members was now counted as seventy-two. A building was constructed on the corner of Florida and Franklin Streets, but the members wanted a new location for the church. They removed the building constructed in 1908 from its foundation and placed it in a new location at the corner of Atlantic Street and Douglas Avenue in the Woodland Heights neighborhood. The church was then called by its current name, Woodland Heights Presbyterian Church.

The original, frame building served the church's needs for 51 years until 1951, when the education and administrative addition was built and dedicated. The congregation used this building for another 50 years, with worship being held in the fellowship hall. In 1960, the old building was dismantled and the material used for various purposes, but the bell that had graced the church was kept in storage. Made of brass, the bell had once graced a Frisco Railroad 4500 Engine. Somehow, the bell made its way to the Frisco Railroad Museum until a member purchased it in 2005. It was kept until a new sanctuary was built in 2009, and was then placed in the church tower where it calls worshippers to service. A steel, Celtic cross graces the new sanctuary. This cross, built by member Scott Mahaffery, was carried to the church on the shoulders of members, hoisted by crane and installed.

The members of this church have accomplished good works beyond what would appear possible because of God's grace and power working through them. The church supports many groups, including Christian Endeavor, a youth group who meet for Bible lessons and fellowship. A Ladies Aid Society, which was started in 1925, continues to meet. A Christian Men's Club was active in the community and Boy Scout Troop 18, which began in 1922, still meets at the church.

Throughout its history, Woodland Heights has been privileged to have pastors who have served and drawn the church together. Greg Esselman, who came to the church in April of 1988, served the longest. He resigned as pastor in June of 2014, after 24 plus years of service.

Woodland Heights belongs to the Presbyterian Church (USA) with national offices in Louisville, Kentucky. Nine United States presidents listed their religion as Presbyterian. Some doubt the placement of Rutherford B. Hayes the 19th president. Though raised as a Presbyterian, references do not list any religion practiced as an adult.

The history and information on the formation of this church is slight and the authors appreciate the assistance of the members, Joseph Han-

Carrying the Celtic Cross for Woodland Heights Presbyterian Church

Raising the Celtic Cross at Woodland Heights Presbyterian Church

Woodland Heights Presbyterian Church, 2017

kins and Dennis George who graciously provided information. In addition, thanks go to other pastors in the area who were able to supply names as contacts to complete this document. The church suffered from declining membership and loss of their pastors, but as of the summer of 2016, a vote of confidence was held by the remaining congregation to continue to keep the church going forward. As of this writing, January of 2017, a pastor has accepted the call to head the church.

Current Information

722 West Atlantic Street
(417) 866-0894
www.whpchurch.com/

Resources Used

History of Woodland Heights Presbyterian Church

Past and Present of Greene County Missouri. Jonathan Fairbanks and Clyde Edwin Tuck, thelibrary.org

Woodland Heights Presbyterian Church Homecoming September 9, 1912

Woodland Heights Presbyterian Church Our History and About Presbyterians

Central Assembly of God, 1907

The history of Central Assembly of God is expansive and rich. It has touched the lives of thousands in Springfield and around the world through its ministries. The church has accomplished much in pursuit of God's purpose, and its beginnings came from two sisters. They laid the foundation for the movement as it exists in Springfield today.

James and Lillie Corum moved their family from Fort Sill, Oklahoma, to a house on Division Street, just beyond the city limits of Springfield. Lillie cared for their four children while James worked for the Frisco Railroad, as did so many others in Springfield. Lillie and the children were excited as they waited for her sister and the children's aunt, Rachel Sizelove, to arrive. Rachel would be traveling to Springfield from California, where she had been attending meetings at the Azusa Street Mission in Los Angeles.

Upon hearing the sound of a taxi wagon coming down Division Street, the children ran to tell their mother that their Aunt Rachel had arrived. Rachel, too, was excited. She was anxious to share the thrill of what she had experienced in Los Angeles and the news of the powerful outpouring of the Holy Spirit at the mission. When she stepped through the doorway, her face was aglow with the news she wanted to share with Lillie and James. As she spoke, she did so in a heavenly language.

Things would never be the same in the Corum household, or in Springfield, once Rachel had shared her news and the two sisters prayed together. In time, Rachel would ignite a movement of Pentecostalism that no one in the humble Corum household could imagine. Talk about Rachel and what she had witnessed in California began to spread, and soon, neighbors were coming to the house to meet with her and hear her story. Rachel would invite them to pray with her. During a session on June 1, 1907, Lillie was filled with the Holy Spirit and was the first person in Springfield to receive this blessing. James had not experienced the Holy Spirit as his wife had and it would be several years before he did, but nonetheless he fully supported all that was taking place.

James and Lillie were dismissed from the church they had been attending for embracing the Pentecostal experience, but they were undaunted. Lillie continued to gather those who would listen to what her sister had witnessed in California. Not all were receptive, but prayer meetings continued in the house on Division Street as well as in tent meetings on Center Street (now Central) throughout the summer of 1907. The neighbors, friends and family who gathered there would become the beginning congregation of what would become Central Assembly of God.

Tents were pitched and revivals held on Center Street that summer. Large crowds attended, including students from Drury College and pastors of denominational churches. Groups of these men were saying that the revivals held in the tent were a terrible thing to do in the name of religion. They wanted to gather a posse and run the Pentecostal people out of town. (They were known as Pentecostal then.) A man from the First Baptist Church persuaded the group to leave the worshippers alone. He said, "If it's not of God, it will soon fall through, but if it is of God, it will stand."

By 1908, services were moved to Bethel Chapel on the southeast corner of Campbell Avenue and Calhoun Street. A traveling minister, L.B. Sly, preached at the Bethel Chapel for a time. There is no further information through research to share in regard to L.B. Sly. Meetings and prayers continued at Bethel Chapel during this time.

In about 1910, another person heard of Lillie Corum and the work she was doing. Her name was Amanda E. Benedict. She had moved to Springfield from Chicago where she had worked with a rescue home for girls. She had also worked in Iowa at a home for children. Shortly after her arrival in Springfield, she met Lillie Corum who was then forming the seed congregation for Central Assembly. Amanda was intrigued with the stories of Azusa Street and Lillie's story of her baptism of the Holy Spirit and wanted the experience for herself. It was not long before she too had the gift of the baptism.

Amanda burned with a desire to have the works of God established in Springfield and flow to the ends of the earth. In April of 1911, she and Lillie Corum received permission to erect a tattered tent that had been donated to them for their meetings. The property where the tent was unfurled was on the northeast corner of Campbell Avenue and Calhoun Street and belonged to a gentleman by the name of Kirby, who owned a saloon on the square. Despite opposition, those that gathered in the many meetings in the tattered tent experienced blessed times of seeking Christ. (As it happens this piece of property is part of the same location where the Central Assembly of God church now stands.)

Amanda Benedict worked tirelessly for Springfield and Central Assembly. She had a vision of a great revival coming to Springfield. She struggled when in her prayers she saw a vision of storm clouds attempting to roll over the city that contained dark powers, which she felt represented the opposition to the Pentecostal movement. For a year she ate nothing but bread and water and prayed for the movement and the spirit of Springfield. The group continued to move around the streets of Springfield erecting their tent on Commercial, Division, and Central Streets.

Temporary quarters were rented on Commercial and Division Streets, and the group returned to the Woodman Hall on Prospect Street for services. By January of 1913, the Bethel Chapel on the southeast corner of Campbell and Calhoun was utilized until a move to a wooden building at Boonville and Calhoun in April of that year. (Amanda Benedict passed away in 1925. She is a tireless symbol for Central Assembly and for the Assembly of God Headquarters.)

James S. Eaton from Eureka Springs, Arkansas, was elected first pastor of the church in 1914, and was followed in the pulpit by Bennett F. Lawrence. Pastor Lawrence stayed with the church until 1917. It was sometime during his tenure that the church moved once more to a building on the corner of Main and Webster. It was also during the time that Bennett F. Lawrence was with the church that they became affiliated with the Assemblies of God Fellowship whose headquarters were in Findley, Ohio.

On New Year's Eve in 1916, Pastor Lawrence was in the pulpit close to midnight. He told those gathered that 1917 could mark the year that the Lord would return, as war was raging in Europe and the world was in turmoil. After services, four young boys walked together to go home and took a shortcut across White City, which was a large amusement park in the city of Springfield. The shortcut took them from Campbell Avenue to Boonville and Division. The amusement park was deserted at this hour, and the boys knew it had a reputation for being an evil place where burlesque was allowed. They wanted to claim the park for the Lord. They knelt and prayed over the block where the amusement park stood and added the next block as well – from Boonville to Campbell and from Division to Calhoun. Today, those same blocks house the Assembly of God Headquarters, bookstore and Central Assembly Church. Little by little, all the land the boys had prayed over became the property of the Assembly.

White City Amusement Park; Assembly of God would later built their headquarters on this land.

The first building for Central Assembly of God

As the crowds began to grow in size, they built a small frame tabernacle on Center Street across from the courthouse. Several men were elected as pastors for short periods throughout the period 1917 through 1920. W.T. Gaston was one of these, and he later served as general superintendent from 1925-1929.

On July 1, 1920, the group dedicated a pleasant white frame building as their church. It stood on the northeast corner of Campbell and Calhoun. This location had been prayed over by Lillie Corum and Amanda Benedict, who received visions about a permanent church being built on this site. Aimee Semple McPherson was scheduled to deliver the opening message at the new church, but the crowd became too large for the building and the service was moved to the downtown convention hall.

In January of 1922, a supply pastor, D.W. Kerr, would serve the church for several months. He became the first president of the Central Bible Institute, which opened in the basement of Central Assembly in October of 1922. The school remained at this location until it had its own campus in North Springfield on North Grant Avenue. The first class graduated in 1925, from a permanent building that had been constructed at the Grant Avenue site.

The General Council of the Assembly of God Headquarters founded Evangel University in 1955. Eighty-seven students attended the first day of classes on September 1st of that year. In 2010, the Assembly of God began an effort to consolidate Central Bible College and the Assembly of God Theological Seminary with Evangel University, as all three were located in Springfield, Missouri. The consolidation was approved in April of 2013, and the new Evangel University was launched in August of 2013.

D.W. Kerr again filled the pulpit at the church in 1925 and 1926. During his time, Central Assembly officially affiliated with the Assembly of God headquarters. Central Assembly Church predates the formation of the Assembly of God headquarters by seven years. New pastors filled the pulpit through 1931, and the church sent out its first missionary to Tibet in 1926.

Disaster struck the church when on December 21, 1929, the white church building burned to the ground. No information into the investigation of the fire was given. Temporary quarters were used for services at the Pythian Hall on Boonville Avenue. By 1930, a church facility complete with a 600-seat auditorium, was built on the site where the church building burned. The auditorium was later used for weddings and midweek services.

Ralph M. Riggs, who received the baptism of the Holy Ghost and the call to the ministry in 1913, was elected to the pulpit in June 1931. He served the church until 1938, after having first come as a supply pastor. He is credited with opening branch churches all across Springfield. There was a branch on the east side of town, known as Praise Assembly, and a northside assembly known as Northeast Assembly, then known as Bethel. On the southside, the branch was known as Calvary Temple. He is credited with spearheading the formation of Evangel College against strong opposition from many members of the Assembly. He later became general superintendent in 1953, and served in that post until 1959.

The church continued to grow with a revival in 1935, with Evangelist Emma Taylor. A program to expand the auditorium and add Sunday School rooms was started. Bert Webb, who later served as assistant general superintendent from 1949 to 1969, filled the pulpit at Central Assembly in June of 1939 until 1943.

Thomas F. Zimmerman, who came later to fill the pulpit at the church, started a radio program titled "Sermons in Songs." He came from Granite City, Illinois, and served for approximately two years. The program was broadcast on KWTO and was adopted by the Assembly of God Headquarters. Other radio programs of the Central

White City Amusement Park property as it looks today.

Assembly were also broadcasted on KWTO. "Words of Life," was the work of Emil A. Balliet who was elected pastor from 1947 until 1952. Also during his tenure, plans were made for the expansion of the church buildings.

The dedication of the new sanctuary at Boonville Avenue and Calhoun Streets was observed on September 15, 1957, and was followed by a host of revivals with many well-known names in the Assembly of God community. Shortly after the dedication, James L. McQueen was elected pastor and he served until forced to resign, due to his health, in 1964. Next at the pulpit was E. Elsworth Krogstad, who was then succeeded by Phillip P. Wannenmacher in 1970.

Phillip Wannenmacher graduated from Central Bible Institute in 1945, and had his first introduction to the Central Assembly church when he came to visit his sister who attended the church. He met his future wife, Betty, who attended Central Assembly and was the daughter of a minister. After a lengthy courtship, carried out over long distances due to Phillip's work in other churches, they married in 1949. After filling positions at various churches around the country, he was invited by the pastoral search committee to Springfield, which ultimately led to his election as senior pastor. He served the church from 1970 to 1995. During his time as pastor, he could see the need for additional space for the church to fulfill its mission to serve the people of Springfield, but there was dissention over the project. A fire on November 3, 1980, burned the West Chapel, which had been erected on the exact location of the old church that had burned in 1929. After the fire, Pastor Wannenmacher could see the focus of the church change and a new three-story nursery/education building was planned and funded. This was paid in part by the proceeds of the insurance money received from the fire.

Reverend Wannenmacher broadcasted a daily television program, "It's a Great Life," on KYTV. In 1990, groundbreaking for a new worship center and education facility was held. The first service in the new

Central Assembly of God, 2017

sanctuary, with a capacity of 2300, was held on January 5, 1992. Dedication was held for a 230-seat chapel and new classrooms, on March 22 and 23 of 1992.

Since the departure of Phillip Wannenmacher, several pastors have occupied the pulpit. As of this writing, Mike McCrary fills the position of Senior Associate Pastor. In April of 2006, a multipurpose hall was dedicated.

It should be noted that the origin of this church was in meetings in a wooden frame house on Division Street with ardent prayers and visions that later became reality. This was the work and devotion of three people, all women, Rachel Sizelove, Lillie Corum and Amanda Benedict.

Current Information

1301 North Booneville
(417) 866-5013
www.centralassembly.org/our-history/

Resources Used

The Sparkling Fountain – Fred T. Corum and Hazel E. Bakewell. Published by Corum & Associates, Inc.

Wikipedia the Free Encyclopedia – Evangel University.

Windows into Central's 100 Years of Ministry – complied and printed by Central Assembly

St. Agnes Catholic Parish, 1908
St. Agnes Cathedral, 1956

Congratulatory letters from Pope Benedict and others in the Catholic faith, along with officials of the state government of Missouri, and the city of Springfield flooded St. Agnes Cathedral on the centennial celebration of its founding, September 8, 2008. The beginnings for the church were surrounded by controversy, but the safety of children and adults was one of the is the reasons the church became a reality.

Arrangements were made by Archbishop Peter Kenrick, of the Diocese of St. Louis, for a resident priest to be assigned. In early March of 1866, Father Francis W. Graham arrived in the city and just days later celebrated what is believed to be the first Mass in the city of Springfield, Missouri. With that humble beginning, the Catholic faith put its stamp on the city. By 1870, immigrants from Ireland and Germany came in large numbers to work and live in the city as the Atlantic Pacific Railroad was being built.

Some of the children of these immigrants attended Catholic school north of the city, and some were welcomed to a small Catholic elementary school called St. Ann's School of Loretto on the south side of the city, beyond the tracks of the Atlantic Pacific Railroad. (The school started in 1906, and was later renamed St. Agnes.)

When the children walked to north-side Catholic schools and to Immaculate Conception Church, it was necessary for them to cross the railroad tracks, which ran along Mill Street. Parents were fearful of the dangers. Approximately 20 passenger trains roared along the tracks each day as they passed through the city. There were now as many as 100 families living south of the tracks and crossing them to attend Mass and other activities at Immaculate Conception Church.

These families began to petition Bishop John Hogan, then the head of the Diocese of Kansas City, for a church to be built south of the tracks for the safety of the children. Ultimately, their requests were granted, but not before the objections of Father John J. Lilly, then pastor of Immaculate Conception Church were resolved.

A temporary meeting place was needed, and the former Central Congregational Church at Walnut and Market Streets was rented for

Dedication of St. Agnes Church, November 24, 1910. Courtesy of St. Agnes Archives

the sum of $40 a month. Father Denis J. O'Driscoll celebrated the first Mass in the newly-formed church in September of 1908.

The name St. Agnes was chosen to honor the Catholic patron of young girls. A stained glass window created in her image graces the church to this day.

Once the temporary church was founded, a committee was formed to search for property to build a permanent home for St. Agnes. The committee deliberated over two locations, and ultimately chose property located at South Jefferson Avenue and Mount Vernon Streets. They decided that the entrance of the church should face Cherry Street. The parcel was purchased for the sum of $10,500.00, and the church stands in this location today. It is interesting to note that electricity, though not prevalent at the time the church was constructed, would be used to illuminate the building, with candles accenting the altar.

The new church building was dedicated Thanksgiving Day, November 24, 1910. A reporter estimated that that 3,000 people were in attendance and filling the floor and choir loft. Many others were unable to gain entrance.

The architectural firm of Miller, Opel, and Torbitt designed the church in the Classical Revival Style. They also designed other landmark buildings in Springfield, such as Landers Theater and the Heer's Department Store.

The ladies of the church raised the money needed to buy an organ for the church. It was said to be the finest in the region and cost the sum of $3,000.00.

Through the years, as the church continued to grow, there were changes to both the interior and the exterior and more property was purchased for expansion. There were changes to correct architectural issues and damage from fire or other elements. New altars were added several times. One altar was carefully removed when a fire in the basement destroyed the floor of the church and allowed the six-ton, marble altar to sag. When the original altar from St. Agnes was replaced in the early 1930s, it was sent to St. Mary's Church in Higginsville, Missouri, to help rebuild that church which had been destroyed by fire.

In 1909, St. Ann's school was moved to the new property, and a new, two-story building for the school was built in 1913, at a cost of $10,000.00. By 1914, five sisters of Loretto were teaching at the school with an enrollment of 175 students.

In 1921, Reverend L. Curtis Tiernan became pastor. He had previously served as an associate pastor of the Immaculate Conception Catholic Church in Springfield and churches in Kansas City. He became a military chaplain in World War I and began a lifelong friendship with Harry Truman. The two met at Fort Sill, Oklahoma, and served in the the same combat company in France. After the war, Father Tiernan

St. Agnes Grade School, April 29, 1921. Note: the cottage to the left was probably the school used from 1909-1913.

("Padre" to the troops) served churches in Kansas City before coming to St. Agnes. He was also appointed dean of the Springfield district in 1922. He returned to active duty as a military chaplain in 1929.

In 1931, three beautiful new altars were installed in the church with the high altar measuring 16 feet wide and 20 feet tall. Hardwood floors for the sanctuary were also installed that year.

Though not documented, it is believed that around 1931, the two bell towers that graced the church at the time of construction were removed. Created of terra cotta masonry, they suffered severe water damage that would need repairs, but instead were removed. The church stands without them to this day.

A private residence was purchased by the church in 1936, and was used as a high school. It was expanded in 1939, with a new building for that purpose, which included a gymnasium. The building was located on the corner of Jefferson Avenue and Cherry Street.

In 1941, one of the buildings vacated by the school became the Springfield USO Club. Troops stationed at Fort Leonard Wood enjoyed socializing, entertainment, and refreshments on Sunday afternoons. The use of the building as a USO club was terminated in 1944. It is believed that approximately 200 parishoners from St. Agnes served during World War II, though no official records of their military service were kept by the church.

In 1954, Christmas Midnight Mass was televised from the church. This was the first time in history such a service had been televised from cameras in Springfield.

In 1956, St. Agnes Church was designated a cathedral when the newly-formed Springfield-Cape Girardeau Diocese was established under the leadership of Pope Pius the XII.

In September of 1958, a High Mass to celebrate the 50th anniversary of the church and the dedication of a new elementary school was held.

In November of 1963, the tragic death of President John F. Kennedy was memorialized with a mass at St. Agnes. The church was filled to capacity with mourners.

In August of 1984, a chapel with a capacity of 75 was added during a major renovation of the church. It would be used for funerals, weddings, daily Mass, and other small gatherings. Extensive renovations were made on all the stained-glass windows in the church, including moving some to new locations within the church. The total cost of this renovation exceeded one million dollars and added many changes to the church interior.

Another renovation occurred in 2003. The cathedral closed and services were held in the school cafeteria. The renovation included many repairs and updates that were necessary, such as new floors, new tile in the vestibule, a new updated sound system, and the oiling of the pews.

In 2004, the original organ purchased by the women of the church in 1910, was replaced. Repairs to the instrument were no longer possible as the manufacturer was no longer in business and parts were not available. The new pipe organ contained 1,333 pipes ranging in size from 1/2 inch to 8 feet tall. The total cost of the organ, including preparation in the church for its placement, was $350,000.00.

September 30, 2007, began the kickoff for many celebrations to honor the centennial of the cathedral.

Many functions and wonderful events have ocurred at this cathedral. The church grew, prospered, and added to its membership. Buildings and athletic fields were completed for the school and church through fundraising projects. A convent for the teaching nuns was built, and the interior of the church was beautified many times with statuary and painted murals.

From its beginning in 1908, St. Agnes has been blessed with pastors that have through their guidance, devotion, hard work and planning brought pride to the city and the church. They are from many diverse backgrounds and served in many other churches throughout the country and Missouri.

In 1891, the nuns added their caring to the health needs of Springfield by assisting in the creation of St. John's Hospital, today known as Mercy Hospital. In 1982, it was proposed that Catholics provide free meals for the poor. Five sisters, known as the "Little Portion Franciscans," volunteered their time. The meals were served in the St. Agnes Elementary School cafeteria to forty people on the very first day it began. The program called "The Kitchen" continues to provide social services to families, youth, and veterans in the city.

Current Information

533 South Jefferson Avenue
(417) 831-3515
www.saintagnescathedral.org/about/parish-history

St. Agnes Catholic Cathedral, 2017

Resources Used

Courtesy of the Greene County Library _ thelibrary.org/lochist/postcard/st_agnescfm

McAlear, Sally Lyons, *South of the Tracks – A Centennial History of St. Agnes Parish Springfield Missouri 1908-2008*

Pastva, Loretta, *The Catholic Churches in Southern Missouri, 1956-2006*

Shank, Lili, *Harry & Padre*, 2016

The Kitchen Inc.org

Wikipedia the Free Encyclopedia – St. Agnes Cathedral (Springfield Missouri)

www.saintagnescathedral.org/about/parish-history

Chapter Seven

1910s

Historical Notes

National and international events had an impact on Missouri and Springfield. In 1914, World War I began in Europe. Although it would be three years before the United States enetered the war, local debates about military preparedness and potential involvement in the international conflict would occupy many levels of society.

Springfield now had 50 miles of paved roads for the increasing number of automobiles. The town now claimed to have 108 manufacturing industries employing 4,443 persons. Electricity came to Springfield in 1910.

Churches Established No Longer Operating

First Freewill Baptist Church, 1914

Churches Currently Operating

Trinity Lutheran Church, 1910
Seventh Baptist Church, 1911
  National Boulevard Baptist Church, 1934
Johnson and Dale Church of Christ, 1911
  Kansas Expressway Church of Christ, 1977
Sunset Baptist Church, 1913
  Northwest Baptist Church, 1935
Westside Baptist Church, 1915
  Immanuel Baptist Church, 1930
Forest Hills Church, 1915
Walnut Street Christian Church, 1947

The Evangelical Lutheran Trinity Church, Unaltered Augsburg Confession, 1910
Trinity Lutheran Church, 1910

Starting from a struggling mission congregation in 1910, Trinity Lutheran grew into a strong, self-sustaining congregation by 1927, even though membership was quite small. Trinity has sponsored and supported two other congregations in Springfield: Redeemer and Faith Lutheran. It also has given its support to St. Paul's in Branson, Zion in Bolivar, and financial help to Hope Lutheran in Republic.

Before these achievements were mastered, there were hard times and disappointments as they struggled to become a great church. Attempts were made to form a congregation in Springfield as early as the 1870s and 1880s, but years would pass before the beginnings of a congregation was formed.

Two men, Reverend Schuest, 1880-1889, and the Reverend Lehn, 1889-1894, came to look at the city of Springfield to determine if there were Lutherans ready to support services. When the Lutherans were invited to join Reverend Schuest for services, the response was "Yes, we shall be there if you permit us to bring our usual keg of beer with us."

As would be expected, Reverend Schuest's invitation was withdrawn under those circumstances. Many Lutherans who had come to Springfield soon left because of the absence of a Lutheran church. They wanted the familiarity of the church for their youth and to bring their children up in the nurture of the scriptures.

There were occasional Lutheran services conducted in Springfield. Reverend Hintz, who was the pastor at Stones Prairie, Missouri, from 1889-1898, conducted services in a building on the northwest corner of College Street and Campbell Avenue. This location was the regular worship site of South Street Christian Church. They also used a Presbyterian Church building at West Walnut Street and Market Avenue. Again, in 1901, a search of Springfield for Lutherans in need or want of a church was in vain.

Finally, in 1907, Reverend V.W. Richter held regular Lutheran services on a monthly basis in two different churches. One was a Presbyterian Church at Broadway and Division, and the other a Seventh Day Adventist Church at Lynn and Main. The sum of $15.00 was paid monthly for the use of the Seventh Day Adventist church. The services were held at 2:00 p.m. to allow the pastor to preach at his home church in Billings, Missouri, and then travel by train to Springfield to conduct services.

No effort was made to organize a congregation until January 9, 1910, when the first Lutheran congregation adopted its name, "The Evangelical Lutheran Trinity Church, Unaltered Augsburg Confession, Springfield, Missouri." At a special meeting presided over by Reverend V.W. Richter, who had conducted the monthly meetings, and Gus Roepke, who served as provisional secretary, three members signed the church's constitution: Otto Rader, Gus Roepke, and Frank Erke. Reverend Richter served the group until accepting a call to a church in Shobonier, Illinois, in 1912.

When Reverend Richter left his church in Billings, Missouri, the congregation began to decline and the mission board requested that the pastor called to serve both churches reside in Springfield. The congregations accepted this and Reverend Fred Hertsmann was installed in November of 1912. Due to family illness, Reverend Emil Recknagel replaced him in March of 1914. Reverend Recknagel was called from his duties as a missionary among the native American Indians in Texas.

The congregation, at the time of Reverend Recknagel's installation, numbered about forty. They still had no permanent place to meet and rented space at a vacant Presbyterian Church at East Elm, which had no pews. Elfindale Academy, a Catholic girls' school had some seats that had originally been used at the St. Louis World Fair in 1904, and the congregation bought fifty of the seats for $25.00. A final move to a Presbyterian church at Benton Avenue and East Locust, that was vacant but well furnished, became their home until a permanent place was found.

In a meeting held April 19, 1914, the congregation reorganized under the name "The Evangelical Lutheran Trinty Congregation, Unaltered Augsburg Confession." Reverend Recknagel resigned in May of 1917, and the post stayed vacant until September of 1917, when A.F. Woker was installed. During this period, services were still delivered in German, but at the urging of the mission board, English began to be used and special means were devised to accommodate those who could not speak the language.

Under Reverend Woker's leadership, the congregation began to grow, and by January 1918, voted to build a sanctuary. A committee was appointed to search for a suitable piece of property. A lot located on the east side of North Jefferson Street was purchased for the sum of $1,900.00. Between the Reverend Woker's effort with sister churches and the congregation, the sum of $1,500.00 was raised and the balance of funds needed was secured by a loan. With the purchase of property and the desire to build a sanctuary, the church needed to become incorporated. This was finalized in November of 1918.

Herman Burgdorf of St. Louis, a German architect, prepared plans for the new church; but funds were needed to complete the project so it would not be doomed to failure. A loan of $8,000.00 was secured with the mission board to be repaid over a period of seven years. The building was then completed at a cost of $12,000.00 with the balance needed for the structure financed by the sale of bonds.

Ground was broken on October 15, 1919, and dedication took place on May 30, 1920. A special celebration was held with the congregations from churches in southwest Missouri invited. The Meinert and Lockwood, Missouri, congregations chartered a special train for their trip. They brought a band along that played as the congregations marched to the site of the church. The church had its first permanent home and boasted 100 baptized souls as its congregation. After the dedication, the ladies aid served meals in the basement.

Transportation played a part in the selection of the property to allow for the growth of the church. There were no paved roads and no buses, and automobiles at this time were still a novelty, but the city of Springfield was equipped with an electric streetcar system. The church property was located between two lines, one on Boonville Avenue and one on Benton Avenue. The hook and ladder at the firehouse was motorized, but the pumper was still horse-drawn and steam operated. People walked where they needed to go.

In January of 1920, the church bought a house at 518 East Lynn Avenue as a suitable home for their pastor, for the sum of $3,500.00. The pastor was to pay rent of $20.00 per month.

Growth made it necessary to form the first church council. The council recommended the establishment of three committees: build-

Trinity Lutheran Church on Jeffeson Street

ing and grounds, auditing and finance, and service and reception. Now the church was well on its way to becoming a fully tested and functioning organization. By October of 1926, the congregation passed a resolution declaring they were self-sustaining and the mission board was dismissed from providing further assistance.

The financial health of the church became stronger, and gifts and services from the faithful contributed to the reduction of the mortgage. The ladies aid made an offer to assume the remaining balance of the money due on the parish house of $1,000.00. The congregation also relinquished the requirement that the pastor pay monthly rent. An organ was donated to the Sunday School, a church choir was financed, and the men's club purchased 100 hymnals. The members flocked to the basement of the church to clean up the damage from a flood. All was going well and the congregation continued to grow. The church celebrated its tenth anniversary with the pastor and the church council planning a special celebration to mark their success. Membership had increased to 153 baptized members with 105 communicant members.

In May of 1935, as plans were being made for the celebration of the 25th anniversary of the formation of the church and the 15th anniversary of the church building, Reverend Woker was hospitalized due to illness and the program was dropped. He returned to his duties in July,

Members of Trinity Lutheran in 1930

but was again hospitalized and lost the battle with his illness on October 20, 1935. Reverend Woker had served the church since September of 1917.

A resolution was adopted with the help of the president of the Western District, Dr. Richard Kretzschmar, to have Reverend G.B. Seboldt of Diggins, Missouri, serve the church until a new pastor could be called by the congregation. Eight names were put forth, and on November 18, 1935, a call was extended to Reverend E.H. Koerber, which he accepted. His installation was on January 26, 1936.

In early 1937, the church sought to obtain the services of a seminary student to canvass Springfield and invite the unchurched to Trinity. A student consented to come, and by April 28, 1941, had made 5,000 calls and found that five-sixths of those contacted were church members, and the others sought church services elsewhere. No new members were added to Trinity and a motion to discontinue the program was adopted in 1941.

The congregation grew to over 200 communicants by 1940, and it was now twenty years since the church was built. The need for additional space was becoming apparent and a committee appointed the church council to investigate the possibilities of enlarging the church. A plan to meet the financial needs for expansion was also needed. The council contacted a St. Louis architect, who suggested a $13,000.00 extension to the church building by adding an additional wing. This proposal lost favor as the cost exceeded what the congregation expected. The council was told to develop a plan that would not exceed $8,000.00. A committee was selected to solicit pledges from the congregation for the funds with a request for a loan of $5,000.00 from the church extension board. However, something intervened; the United States entered World War II. The church extension board advised that the construction should wait. This was a wise decision as non-war related construction was brought to a standstill due to lack of materials.

In January of 1942, after the United States had declared war, the pledges that were outstanding for the addition were collected and placed in a building fund until the construction could get underway. Meanwhile, Trinty participated in many projects brought about by the war. They supported the 43 young men from their congregation who were in the service, by sending letters and holding special prayer services for their safety.

As the 25th anniversary of the church building approached, a special service was held to mark the occasion. The congregation now numbered 350 souls with a communicant membership of 235, and 70 children who were being taught by nine teachers in Sunday School. Great stress was placed on the youth of the church, as they would, as adults, assume the responsibilities of the church and of the community.

By 1946, the membership had grown to numbers large enough that the assistance of another pastor was needed. The church council approved this and a student pastor was hired from September until May at a salary of $100.00 per month. A shortage of students for the project created a delay, which lasted until 1955. Vicar Raymond Mack then came to Trinity, and also served St. Paul's mission congregation in Branson.

The congregation was again ready to pursue a building program by 1947, and a new committee was elected to explore the church's options. The recommendation was to expand at the Jefferson location, but property that would suit their needs was unattainable, as the woman who lived on and owned the property had no interest in selling. This was disappointing to the congregation and a search for a possible site for a new church was started.

One of the criteria considered for access to public transportation. Walking and streetcars, the predominant mode of transportation in the past, were replaced by bus lines and personal automobiles. Since there was considerable interest in a parochial school, the new property needed to have sufficient room for that endeavor. In March of 1950, multiple lots at the corners of Bennett Street and Holland Avenue were found with a total area of 2.8 acres. It took great imagination to visualize a church on the weed-choked parcel that had been used as a rubbish dump. However, the view from the church would be Phelps Grove Park, and a bus line was nearby. The property was bought for $10,000.00.

The first order of business was to pave Holland Avenue. The people who lived in the neighborhood were pleased with this major improvement, and Trinty would pay $5,000.00 as their share of the cost. Availability of building materials was sluggish due to the effects of the war, but other work and activities at the church continued. A Boy Scout Troop was organized which continues to this day. The 30th Anniversary of the troop was celebrated in 1984.

Trinity Lutheran Church at 1415 South Holland, was dedicated on June 7, 1953.

By 1951, the scarcity of building materials began to ease, and with the property purchased, it was time to begin planning the new church. By July of 1951, architect Richard P. Stahl was selected to create plans for a building with a seating capacity of 450. The completed plans received unanimous approval for a contemporary design. Construction bids were solicited and, as would be expected, the cost exceeded what had been anticipated. Elimination of some items that could wait until a later date brought the cost of the building down to an acceptable level of $138,800.13 and construction began. To cover the cost of the building, the church issued bonds for $70,000.00, with the balance of the funds taken from the church treasury and pledges from the members.

On Sunday evening, August 3, 1952, Pastor E.H. Koerber preached from 1 Chronicles 22:19 "Build Ye the Sanctuary of the Lord." The next morning excavation of the property began. On June 7, 1953, all the planning, dreams, and aspirations climaxed as the time of dedication for the new building arrived. Open house was held for tours of the facility and the sister congregations came to congratulate Trinity. At a special service, donations were requested to help the church pay for a ceiling for the basement, which had not been included in the original construction cost.

A new chapter for the church in its new facility would begin, and plans for the future had already been laid. Sunday School rooms and a new parsonage were needed, and the church began growing into its new space with 600 souls in the congregation and 408 communicant members.

In 1957, Vacation Bible School was started on a trial basis. The women of the ladies aid accepted the burden of planning and the cost for the summer activity. At a congregational meeting, it was reported that attendance had been 158 children, of which 27 were not Lutheran and 106 had perfect attendance. The cost of the program was $332.91. A resolution was adopted to continue the program each summer.

The church now pursued two plans: establishing a Christian day school, and acquiring land for the establishment of another mission church. These responsibilities were placed in the hands of a building committee for action. The committee, after consulting with the mission board of the Western District, was given the support for a new mission church. The Springfield Chamber of Commerce provided a map that projected the growth expected for the city. Areas in the south, southeast, southwest and northwest parts of Springfield were highlighted as having the most growth potential by 1980. Several officials from the western district of the mission board came to Springfield to review the areas, but the ultimate decision for the site was left to the church council. A committee to spearhead the formation of the new congregation was appointed, and property with an area of six acres was purchased for the sum of $18,000.00 at Woodland and South Grant Avenue. Trinty paid for the cost of street paving and for bringing utilities to the property.

Trinity released 48 members to form the nucleus of the congregation for this mission church, which was named Redeemer Lutheran Church. The first service was held June 18, 1960, in the assembly hall of Sherm Lollar Lanes on West Sunshine, which became the church's temporary meeting place. The sanctuary was dedicated in January of 1969, and the congregation became self-supporting with membership at 451 souls. Trinity retired debt that had been accrued while supporting Redeemer Lutheran in 1968.

In 1956, Trinity celebrated the 20th anniversary of its pastor, Reverend Koerber. A surprise program was presented which featured a "This is Your Life" format. This also marked Reverend Kroeber's 30th year in the ministry. Reverend Koerber announced his resignation and retirement in 1966, with delivery of his farewell sermon in October, after 31 years as Trinity's pastor. A new pastor, Reverend Carl W. Heilman, was installed in February 1967. Membership was reported at 1037 souls with 787 as communicants and 250 baptized children.

The superintendent of Sunday School reported enrollment had increased by 24 new members even while 33 children had been released to the Redeemer Mission Church. New educational facilities were needed for the growing numbers. Plans for increasing the space had been discussed, but never formulated. Now necessity pushed the need forward, and the buildings were completed in 1963. Trinty held its first parochial school kindergarten with an enrollment of 18 pupils in 1962. The kindergarten continued until Springfield Public Schools incorporated kindergarten in its curriculum in 1966. Trinity discontinued classes at that time.

After much discussion, air conditioning and a new furnace were installed in the church in 1970, for a total cost of $21,000.00. The finance committee created a campaign to secure the funds.

In 1974, Trinity again worked on efforts to support a mission church in Bolivar, Missouri. Pastor Heilman and other members of the congregation made the weekly trip for worship services, which were held at 7:30 p.m. In 1975, the Missouri District Mission Board called for a reverend as missionary-at-large to serve the church, as interest and dedication by the Bolivar residents grew.

In August of 1974, the long range planning committee of the church called for anyone interested in forming a new congregation. Twenty-eight people attended the meeting representing 55 souls. The committee met with the board of missions who advised them to proceed with the plans for a new mission. The new church would be called Faith Lutheran. Officers were elected, a constitution was drafted, and a temporary place of worship was sought. Sunday, October 20th, the first services were held in Bakers' Union Hall, 336 East Commercial Street. Land was purchased and a missionary-at-large was called by the Missouri District to serve at Faith in Springfield and the group in Bolivar, now called Zion. Faith Lutheran held its last service at Bakers' Union Hall in December of 1976, and dedicated their new building in February of 1977, with 152 souls as its membership.

At Trinity, a fifteen-member committee presented its recommendation to employ a director of youth and education and a pastoral assistant. Statistics for membership at the close of 1974 were 926 communicants and 201 baptized children for a total of 1,127.

The Lutheran Church Missouri Synod celebrated its 125th anniversary in 1972. Emphasis was placed on the role of the church in the world. Trinty planned a special observance to recognize this synodical milestone and contributed to the synod fundraising goals with a special offering.

A devastating tornado came through Springfield on April 29, 1983, and destroyed the sanctuary of Trinity's daughter church, Redeemer Lutheran. Trinity adjusted all their service times and activities and shared their facility with Redeemer through this crisis. By June 5, the damage to Redeemer's education building had been repaired and could be used for services.

In compliance with a directive from the synod, a circuit convocation (or meeting) of members and pastors to further the work and goals of the synod was to be held. The first convocation of the Springfield Circuit was held in October 1984 at Trinity. The agenda was to gather and discuss various phases of the work pursued by the synod and to share in the formation of new churches. Thirteen from the Springfield Circuit attended.

In January of 1984, a new mission church was begun in Republic, Missouri. The first service was held in a small, rented house on Highway 60 and Harrison Street. The name selected for the church was Hope Lutheran. In June, Trinity released 24 from its membership to help form the congregation. Trinity congregation presented the mission with a check for $2,500.00 to help with expenses. This first meeting place was quickly outgrown and three surplus classrooms were moved to a lot owned by the district in Republic. After much volunteer labor from members and friends, the structure was completed and the first services in the new church were held October 7, 1984.

As the church neared its 75th anniversary in 1985, the congregation was saddened to learn that Pastor Heilman, who had been with the church since 1967, would be retiring, and a new shepherd would come to guide them as they moved forward. At the close of 1984, congregation numbers were reported as 1,016 souls, 825 communicants, and 191 baptized souls. Trinity Lutheran Church continued achieving more good works through their 100th anniversary in 2010 and to the present.

Trinty Lutheran is the product of men and women who labored hard and created much, which tells us of their unfailing devotion to the glory of God. They have shown their spiritual dedication and spread

Trinity Lutheran Church, 2017

the word by meeting the need for missions, and helping to build the vibrant city of Springfield. The projection for their future will be a magnification of their history for the generations to come and the continuation of the glory of God.

Current Information

1415 South Holland Avenue
(417) 866-5878
www.trinity-springfield.org

Resources Used

Trinty Lutheran Church 75 Years in Review – Walsworth Publishing Company, Marceline, Mo. (Acknowledgement : Contributions to this volume were made by church members at the request of the 75Th Anniversary Committee.)

www.trinity-springfield.org

Seventh Baptist Church, 1911
National Boulevard Baptist Church, 1934

Seventh Baptist Church at the corner of Baline Street and National Avenue

Boulevard Baptist Church, ca. 1930s

On July 25, 1911, a tent revival began in the area of what is now National Boulevard and Commercial Street. As a result, there were 44 professions of faith. On August 14, 1911, a Missionary Baptist Church was organized at that location. It was known as the Seventh Baptist Church and became a member of the Greene County Baptist Association. On September 24, 1911, E.T. Sloan became the first pastor. The church met in rented halls until a building was constructed at the corner of Baline Street and National Avenue in 1914. The church celebrated the burning of the debt note in 1919.

In 1924, the church became known as the National Boulevard Baptist Church, later shortened to Boulevard Baptist Church. Over the course of the next two decades, improvements were made to the church building. Frontage and classrooms were added to the back of the building.

Continued outreach and growth with new organizational actvities required consideration of new facilities. In 1959, the church voted to construct a new auditorium and education building. Construction was completed and the new facilities were first used on Easter of 1960. By 1970, the church was again debt free.

A new education wing was added in 1975. The large white cross near the building is an everpresent witness to the community of the church's purpose and mission.

The church location on North National Avenue found the surrounding area becoming sparse in residential population. Church membership had declined, with church families scattered all over the city. In 1975, the widening of National Avenue to four lanes required the auditorium to be torn down.

National Boulevard Baptist Church, 1984

In March 1998, representatives of Boulevard Baptist Church, Washington Avenue Baptist Church, and Drury University met to consider the possiblity of Boulevard selling their property. Some discussions had been held during the previous two years when the church had discussed the possibility of relocation. After much discussion and prayer, the church voted on January 13, 1999 to accept Drury's offer of $720,000 for the property and to relocate the church to property on Eastgate Avenue. The twelve-acre property belonged to the Council of Churches and was purchased for $175,000. Drury offered an incentive to move out early with an additional $75,000 and a six percent loan on the ensuing building debt. The church was also able to temporarily use the Drury campus facilities until the new church was completed. Groundbreaking was held on April 2, 2000, and the first services in the new building were on Easter Sunday, April 15, 2001.

Current Information

1030 South Eastgate Avenue
(417) 881-1070
www.boulevardbaptistchurch.net

Resources Used

www.boulevardbaptistchurch.net

National Boulevard Baptist Church, 2017

Johnson and Dale Church of Christ, 1911 Kansas Expressway Church of Christ, 1977

Authors' Notes: The origin of the Church of Christ in Springfield, Missouri, is a mystery of confusing pieces of a puzzle. There are over five Churches of Christ in the city limits. Most of their actual establishments in the city are undocumented. There were divisions among the membership and new churches resulted. In the history of the Kansas Expressway Church of Christ (www.keococ.org/history.htm), they have a summarized history of the activities of the early Churches of Christ in Springfield prior to the actual establishment of their present church. It is important to note those activities. To meet the criteria for inclusion in the qualifying list, we will note the official establishment of this as one continuous church within the city limits.

The earliest activity within the city limits of Springfield began with a brush arbor meeting held in 1832 at the corner of St. Louis Street and Kimbrough Avenue. From that meeting, a congregation led by Brother Joel H. Haden met in a log cabin courthouse on the town square in 1834. Two years later they moved into Joseph Roundtree's log school at the corner of Main Street and Fulbright Road (College Street).

A second group mentioned was the Walnut Hill Church established in 1882 on land donated by Alexander Clapp. In 1899-1890, both groups became divided over the use of musical instruments in the church. Various factions within the churches split, and there is no clear record of all of their locations. It is recorded that the earlier group constructed a

Kansas Expressway Church of Christ, 2017

building on the corner of Washington and Division Streets in 1899. The Walnut Hill group moved in 1912, to the farm of Brother O.L. Hardin and used a building there for worship. In 1986, this group merged with the Scenic and Weaver group to form the Sunset Church of Christ.

In 1910 there was a tent meeting held on the southwest corner of Boonville and Central Streets. It was sponsored by the Ebenezer Church of Christ. The next year, 1911, a new building was constructed on the north corner of North Johnson and West Dale Streets. It became known as the Johnson and Dale Church of Christ.

In 1977, the Johnson and Dale group moved to the southeast corner of north Kansas Expressway and Talmage Street (current location). The name was then changed to the Kansas Expressway Church of Christ.

Current Information

2540 North Kansas Expressway
(417) 869-2284
www.kecoc.org/history

Resources Used

www.kecoc.org/history

Sunset Baptist Church, 1913
Northwest Baptist Church, 1935

We had hoped to include more information about this church. Yet, after repeated contact attempts, the church has not responded to our requests for information on their organizational history. We have found some limited information from secondary sources that we have included.

The church was organized by six people in 1913. A small frame building was constructed in one day just north of West Atlantic Street on north Meredith Street. Services were held that evening and it was named "Sunset Chappell" because it was completed by sunset and the pastor was Rev. Chappell. They disbanded briefly in 1919, joining with Hamlin Memorial Baptist Church. In one month, they returned to the church building as a mission of Hamlin Memorial. In November, after four months, they were ready to assume reorganization as a church with nine members. By the end of that year they had 28 members.

In 1921, the church purchased a lot on the corner of Lexington and Lee Streets. A basement building was completed in 1922. Church organizations were created and actively served the church and community. In 1935, the name was changed to the Northwest Baptist Church. By 1944, a new church building was completed and covered the basement. Church expansion was made in 1949, with improvements on the church grounds.

Church growth required additional education space and a new education building was completed by Easter Sunday, 1952. Membership

Northwest Baptist Church, 1984

Northwest Baptist Church, 2017

had increased to over 350 members. Improvements were made to the nursery area and music program with the addition of new instruments.

Sadly, on October 28, 1978, the church building was destroyed by arsonists. The group met for six months in the old auditorium of the Broadway Baptist Church. In 1979, the church purchased the property of the East Avenue Baptist Church. The building was remodeled.

Current Information

3075 West Norton Road
www.nwbcspringfield.com/our-story

Resources Used

Bartee, Wayne C., *Greene County Baptist Churches, 1838-1984*
Moser, Arthur Paul, *Churches of Greene County, MO*, 1984
www.nwbcspringfield.com/our-story

Westside Baptist Church, 1915
Immanuel Baptist Church, 1930

Westside Baptist Church, ca. 1910s

Like many of the early 1900s churches in Springfield, Immanuel began as a mission of Grant Avenue Baptist Church in the west of the city. In the summer of 1909, a tent revival on Eagle Street, just south of Nichols, led to the creation of a Sunday School and worship services. A rented house was used in the winter months. In 1910, property was purchased on the corner of what is now Scott and LaFountaine Streets. A 24'x40' church building was constructed with volunteer labor.

The first services were held in the new building in the fall of 1910. It is noted that there were very few cars in Springfield at this time, and most attendeees arrived by horse and buggy or on foot. Electricity came to Springfield in 1910. In September 1912, a 26-day revival was held resulting in 65 candidates for baptism.

The church grew steadily and was organized as West Side Baptist Church in 1915, with 122 charter members. Many of the earliest historical records of the church were lost in a home fire.

Immanuel Baptist Church, ca. 1950s

Immanuel Baptist Church, ca. 1970s

As with other churches during the challenging Depression years of the 1930s, the Greene County Baptist Association was able to provide needed financial assistance. The church also developed creative methods for providing membership relief funds as well as working to eliminate the church indebtedness.

The 1940s brought new growth and a need for additional space. The church, like many others, supported the war efforts through prayers and the purchase of war bonds during this time. In 1947, the church voted to build a new Carthage stone building. It measured 55'x84' with a full basement. The Home Mission Board provided assistance with a $25,000 construction loan. The first services were held in the new building on August 12, 1948.

The 1950s found the church expanding its music, missions and education programs. Materials were purchased to enhance worship experiences through use of hymnbooks and musical instruments.

Continued outreach and growth in the next two decades created a need for new space. The church sponsored a mission, which became the Homeland Baptist Church in 1961. In April 1963, a new sanctuary was completed and the old facility remodeled for use as a youth building. Improvements were made on the church grounds. The first church office was constructed and equipment purchased. A new church sign was erected.

The church and parsonage had air conditioning installed in the 1970s. A church bus was also purchased for outreach in the com-

Immanuel Baptist Church, 1984

Immanuel Baptist Church, 2017

munity. Church incorporation was completed in 1978. New, age-group ministries were created and additional church equipment was purchased.

The 1980s and 1990s found the church making facility improvements and upgrades. Mission programs expanded and additonal support for Southwest Baptist University was initiated. Interest in exploring the possibility of a new family life center was started.

In the early 2000s, plans were developed and finances arranged for a new $400,000 family life center. It was "christened" on December 31, 2002. A number of special offerings for mission projects were collected and disbursed.

A brief overview of the church's statistics shows the following information:

The 1915 membership included 130 members; the peak was reached in 1966 with 1,324 members.

The 1930 property value was $3,500; in 1973 it was $285,000; and in 2005, it was $2,556,000.

More importantly, over the years, the church emphasis on missions and service has seen visible results. The church has ordained and sent out 14 ministers, a home missionary and a foreign missionary.

Current Information

1931 West Nichols Street
(417) 869-7990
www.ibcspringfield.org/

Resources Used

Bartee, Wayne C., *Greene County Baptist Churches, 1838-1984*

Immanuel Baptist Church: Celebrating the Past... Energizing the Present...Anticipating the Future. April 2, 2006

Moser, Arthur Paul, *Churches of Greene County, MO*, 1984

Personal interview with the pastor

www.ibcspringfield.org/

Forest Hills Christian Church, 1915
Walnut Street Christian Church, 1947

Forest Hills Church, 1917

Walnut Street Church, 1947

Walnut Street Christian Church was organized in August of 1915. It was first called the Forest Hills Christian Church. The history of its beginning starts as far back as 1902, when it was known as the Christian Endeavor Union, and meetings were held at the Benton Avenue Methodist Church. The Christian Endeavor Union is a non-denominational group started in 1881, in Portland, Maine, and geared towards youth to promote an earnest Christian life. The group was primarily a Sunday School, which met on Sunday afternoon in the old Gulf School building on West Olive Street.

In 1903, the Christian Endeavor Group asked the South Street Christian Church to take charge of the group. Shortly after Mr. and Mrs. W.R. Self, members of South Street Church, came to the Sunday School. Mrs. Self (Francis), would transport youth with her horse and buggy to and from Drury University where some of the Sunday School attendees were students. Drury University is a private, liberal arts school started as Drury College in Springfield in 1873.

In 1911, the Gulf School building burned, and thereafter, services were held in a two-room building until a frame building could be built.

Walnut Street Church, 1970s

Services were held before the building was completed and it is said that the only way to enter or leave the building was by way of a 2 feet x 12 feet board that was 15 feet long and was placed with one end in a window and the other on the ground. The children were said to use this as a slide as they left the building.

The original building used by Forest Hills Church was known as the chicken coop.

Mrs. Self bought a lot at 1917 West Olive Street and a new building was constructed on the lot in one day. There is no indication of the date when the lot was purchased. The building was a frame tabernacle 15 feet square called the "Chicken Coop." Three sides of this building, the east, south and west, were hinged so they could be lifted to increase the size of the building by about 8 feet on the three sides. The building had backless seating made from 2 feet x 12 feet planks. At first grass was the only floor, but a floor was added after three months. As winter approached, the east and west sides were raised and closed in with boards with two 4-light barn sashes placed on each side. (A barn sash is a window meant for a temporary structure.) Mrs. Self donated a 26-inch box stove and firewood was bought from farmers south of the city. In the summer, the south side of the building was raised for cooling.

Only two men attended Gulf Sunday School. If they were not in attendance, the women would take over their duties acting as superintendent and assuming their other duties. Mr. A.T. Mahaney would preach there on Wednesday nights and sometimes on a Sunday, and would take whatever was raised in the collection as payment.

In August of 1915, Forest Hills Christian Church was organized with thirteen charter members. (Through research and inquiries there is no information found to explain the origin of the Forest Hills name.) This organization took place while still using the "Chicken Coop" for their meetings. In about 1916, new building construction began on West Olive Street. The men of the church staked out the building on Thanksgiving while the women prepared lunch. After lunch, all gathered in the yard and Mrs. Self removed the first shovelful of dirt and then each woman, child and man removed a shovelful. They sang hymns, offered prayer, and told of their hopes for the new church. The building was staked out to measure 301 feet x 501 feet and was finished by the men in their spare time.

During construction, a cyclone struck the building and pushed the frame out of alignment. The frame was pushed back to be erect but was always slightly out of plumb, even though steel rods were used to hold it until the siding could be installed.

The first service was held in the new building in the spring of 1917, though it was not quite complete. The old building, the "Chicken Coop," was used as a woodshed for several years after it had served its purpose as a meeting place.

The first pews for the church were crudely made from 2 foot x 8 foot planks until more appropriate seating could be made. As time allowed, the men of the church would gather to build and paint pews. The First Christian Church, when it disbanded, donated $1,000.00 in cash to Forest Hills, which helped to complete the interior of the church. They also were given pews, a pulpit and hymnbooks from the disbanded church. Pews from Forest Hills were, in turn, donated to a small, country church that was just getting started.

Thursday nights during the summer, the church would hold open houses. These gatherings were used as a way to communicate how the church was doing and what more needed to be done to help the church and the community. The meetings were well attended by perhaps 150 people, which made for standing room only. Sandwiches and a beverage, and occasionally ice cream, were served after the meeting.

The church continued to grow and in 1932, it was decided that a larger building was needed to accommodate the growing membership. The new building was finally realized in 1945 and is still in use today. Additional property immediately adjoining the church was purchased for a parking lot, and the present education building was constructed in 1960 and dedicated in 1965.

In 1949, a group of members became dissatisfied with the missionary policies of the church and wanted the church to be independent of any organization. No resolution for the disagreement was found and it is reported that the dissenting members were locked out of the church and formed a new church, Parkview Christian, located on South Campbell. Walnut Street Church is part of the Disciples of Christ, headquartered in Indianapolis, Indiana. Under this organization, each church has a governing board and acts independently of the Indiana headquarters, but adheres to the missionary policies of the Indiana headquarters.

For ten or twelve years, the church had a program called "Hang Time." It was designed as an after-school program geared to keep the children occupied and out of trouble. The program expanded to include adults, and then an evening meal was prepared and served. Parts of the church's congregation were people of little means and the

Walnut Street Christian Church, 2017

evening meal was well received. A group home close to the church was particularly grateful for these meals. The meals were prepared and served in a kitchen in the basement of the church, but a severe storm one January flooded the basement and the program was discontinued. The cost to repair the damage was too great for the church to bear and those who were donating their time to cook were ready to retire, due to their age.

The church, as of 2016, has been together as a congregation for over 100 years. Membership rolls in the church show approximately 150 people and Sunday services are usually attended by 65 or 70. The church uses the following quote as its motto: "A grace place where imperfect people experience the perfect love of God."

Current Information

2201 West Walnut Street
www.walnutstreetchristian.com/index.html

Resources Used

Moser, Paul and Smith, Leana Mae. *Celebrating 100 Years As a History of Walnut Street Church*, 2015

Personal interview with church board president

Conclusion

The obvious question that is asked in such a study is, "What is the oldest church in Springfield?" The answer to that question requires some defining terms. If by "oldest church building," the answer would be the Methodist-Episcopal Church of 1883. If by "oldest, continuous, unchanged, denominational church in the city," the answer would be the Cumberland Presbyterian Church of 1844. Using the definition of "oldest, continuous, unchanged, denominational church in the city," the top three would be:

Cumberland Presbyterian Church, 1844
First Baptist Church, 1852
Christ Episcopal Church, 1859

Today, the number of churches within the current city limits totals about 255. Listed in categories by ChurchFinder.com, the numbers by denominations are as follows:

Baptist Churches	84
Bible Churches	5
Catholic Churches	6
Christian Churches	32
Episcopal Churches	8
Evangelical Churches	9
Hispanic Churches	2
Lutheran Churches	7
Methodist Churches	20
Non-Denominational Churches	7
Orthodox Churches	1
Pentecostal Churches	43

Presbyterian Churches	11
Spirit-Filled Churches	20

This list is not complete, as several other denominations and churches are not included.

It is amazing that among those are thirty-nine churches that qualify as over one hundred years old, in the current city limits and still active. The 216 churches established within the last one hundred years demonstrate the growth of the city, as well as the growth and outreach of those earliest churches.

If the church is defined as a center of worship and ministry in the name of God, then Springfield is truly blessed. As the city continues to identify social and economic needs within the city, local governmental organizations are understanding the need to cooperate with churches in helping to meet those needs. May God look with favor on those who seek to serve Him in our city.

Acknowledgments

The inspiration for this project was the encouragement of Carlene Withers, who was the caretaker of the collection of materials gathered by local Springfield resident, Bob Bowers. Carlene also helped in the original research for this book beginning in January of 2015. The project was put on hold during the fall of 2015, while other priorities occupied the attention of the author. In 2016, Carlene was unable to continue in her research. It became necessary to find a partner in the research and writing. After an appeal was made at a local writer's group meeting, Cecelia Chittenden expressed her interest and offered her services. As a team, it has been a very positive and productive, collaborative effort.

In the very beginning of this project, it was anticipated that a smaller number of churches would fit the criteria established. After the much larger number of churches was discovered, it became necessary to rely on others to assist with the research and gathering of materials. Several individuals offered their assistance with personal contacts in some of the churches. Among these were Ann Willingham, Steve Sherrill, and Mike Haynes, Director of Greene County Baptist Association. We also wish to acknowledge all of those within the 39 churches who aided us with time and the materials to complete this work.

Artwork for the book was provided from several sources. Many of the churches had centennial books made available to us for our use. The personal files of Robert Bowers also contained several important photos. Line drawings of some of the Baptist churches were drawn by Doris Waddell in 1984. Paul Bass personally took current photos of each church in February 2017.

Several individuals have offered their great service in proofreading and editing the original manuscript. Many thanks go to Jan Bass, Gayths Suits, Beverly Burchett and Sally Lyons McAlear for their hours of work to improve the book. Dr. Wayne Bartee was responsible for offering the requested title for the book.

Doug Sikes, Publisher of Acclaim Press, has been a wonderful friend and encourager. His advice and professional suggestions have added to the final publication of this book. The staff at Acclaim Press, in particular, Monica Burnett and Randy Baumgardner, has also been very helpful in the creation and promotion of this book.

Resources

Books

Bartee, Wayne C. *A History of the First Baptist Church, Springfield, Missouri, 1852-1977*, published in 1977

Bartee, Wayne C. *Greene County Baptist Churches in Ministry*, 1838-1984

Bartee, Wayne C. *An Unofficial History of the First Baptist Church of Springfield, Missouri, 1978-2002*, Dogwood Printing: Ozark, MO, 2002

Boyle, Shanna and March, Julie. *Crossroads at the Spring, A Pictorial History of Springfield, Missouri*, The History Museum for Springfield-Greene County, Donning Company Publishers: Virginia Beach, Virginia, 1997

Corum, Fred T. and Bakewell, Helen E. *The Sparkling Fountain*. Windsor, Ohio: Corum and Associates, Inc., 1989

Dark, Harris & Phyllis. *Springfield of the Ozarks, An Illustrated History*, Windsor Publications, Inc., 1981

Fairbanks, Jonathan and Tuck, Clyde Edwin. *Past and Present of Greene County Missouri, Volume 1*, A.W. Bowen and Company: Indianapolis, Indiana, 1915

Meyer, Duane and Arnold, V. Marie. *A Brief History of First and Calvary Presbyterian Church, Springfield*, Missouri, 1987

Moser, Arthur Paul. *Churches of Greene County, MO*, 1983

Moser, Arthur Paul. *Some Churches of Springfield, Missouri*, 1983

Roberts, Anita L. *Images of America, Springfield, 1830-1930*. Charleston, South Carolina: Arcadia Publishing, 1930

Places of Worship in Springfield, Missouri and the Surrounding Area. Springfield Area Council of Churches and the Springfield Ministerial Alliance, 1997

The Churches of Springfield, Missouri. Springfield Area Council of Churches and the Springfield Ministerial Alliance, 1985

Websites

campbellumc.org
churchfinder.com/churches/mo/springfield
religioustolerance/org/rlds
springfieldsynagogue.org
thelibrary.org/lochist/historicalsites/9.cfm
truthforsaints.com/denomination_history/ denomination_history
yourgraceplace.org/our-history

Newspaper/Magazine Articles

Assemblies of God Heritage, Vol. 3, No. 4, Winter 1983-84

Interviews

Immanuel Baptist Church
Marshall, John, Second Baptist Church
Switzer, Raymee, First and Calvary Presbyterian Church, February 19, 1:30 p.m.

Other Materials

Black Families of the Ozarks, Volumes One and Two. Greene County Archives Bulletin Number Forty-Five, 2001. Greene County
City Map and Street Guide, Springfield, Missouri, Springfield Chamber of Commerce, 1955
Clerk's Office
Glenn W. Gohr, Reference Archivist, Flower Pentecostal Center, Springfield, MO, January 15, 2015, email exchanges
Growth of A City, Springfield, Capital of the Great Ozark Empire, Springfield Chamber of Commerce, April 28, 1942
Historical Sites of Springfield, Missouri, Springfield Historical Site Board, Bicentennial Issue, June 23, 1975
Springfield Greets You, Springfield Chamber of Commerce
Telephone Company, churches
Telephone Directory, Springfield, MO, March 1938, Southwestern Bell

About the Authors

Paul William Bass was born in Independence, Missouri. He graduated from William Chrisman High School, Southwest Baptist College and Midwestern Baptist Theological Seminary. He married Jan Smashey in 1969. He served in full-time church staff positions for nineteen years. In 1990-2007, he served at Ouachita Baptist University in Arkadelphia, Arkansas as director of student activities and held various adjunct teaching positions. He became the intercollegiate debate coach with OBU debaters winning three national championships. He took early retirement in 2007, and in that year received the Isocrates Distinguished Debate Coach Award from the International Public Debate Association. During that time in Arkansas, he served in several interim pastor positions and became a bivocational pastor at Anchor Baptist Church for twelve years.

He began his writing career in 2007 with publication of *No Little Dreams: Henry Garland Bennett, Educator and Statesman*. He received the Henry Bennett Distinguished Fellow Award from Oklahoma State University. In 2008 his second book in the Bennett trilogy, *Fellow Dreamers: Oklahoma, Education and the World* was published. The third book in the Bennett trilogy, *Touching the Dream: Point Four*, was published in 2009. That year he was commissioned by Oklahoma State University to write a history of their School of International Studies, entitled *Legacy, Leadership and Learning*. In 2011, he published two religious works from his pastoral experience, *In Jesus' Names* and *Minor Characters of the Bible*. In 2012, he published *Robert S. Kerr: Oklahoma's Pioneer King*. For the Kerr book, he received the 2013 Missouri Writer's Guild First Place President's Award and the 2013 Walter Williams Major Work Award. In 2013, he published *Grace through Tolerance*. In 2014, he completed the autobiographical work of *Me and Church*.

In 2015, a four-year project was published as *The History of Fort Leonard Wood, Missouri*. The book received the 2017 First Prize Walter Williams Major Work Award from the Missouri Writers Guild.

Paul and Jan are retired and living in Willard, Missouri. His email address is bassp@obu.edu.

Cecelia Marriott Chittenden was born the youngest of six children in Pinellas County, Florida and the youngest of four girls. Her family raised and raced Greyhounds in Florida for over 60 years.

She went to Mildred Helms Elementary, Largo Junior High School and graduated from Largo High School in 1962. She married her husband, Abram, in 1965 and shortly after moved to California for his career. Her husband's career offered multiple opportunities for living in different parts of the country. They settled in Colorado for 30 years where a long time hobby of collecting and studying antiques culminated in Cecelia opening an antique store in Denver. They moved to Missouri in 2010.

Raising three children, working and other obligations kept Cecelia from completing a novel she began writing in 1976, but once in Missouri she picked up the novel and after 30 years it has now become a trilogy titled "Pelicans Haven". Books one and two of the planned trilogy are published and book three will be published in 2018. Cecelia has also contributed to two anthologies that at this time remain unpublished. She is also working on other fiction projects, which she hopes to publish in the future.

Index

D

E

F

G

S

T

U

Index of Churches, Missions